MW01077761

THE MYSTERY OF JOY

PETER KREEFT

The Mystery of Joy

IGNATIUS PRESS   SAN FRANCISCO

Cover photo: © iStock/User5dc95804_908

Cover design by Enrique J. Aguilar

© 2025 by Ignatius Press, San Francisco
All rights reserved
ISBN 978-1-62164-745-4 (PB)
ISBN 978-1-64229-329-6 (eBook)
Library of Congress Control Number 2024950098
Printed in the United States of America ∞

CONTENTS

Introduction   11
1 The Need for This Book   13
2 What Is Joy?   16
3 Joy Is Not in Us; We Are in Joy   18
4 C. S. Lewis' Mistake about Joy   21
5 The Last Commandment of the Last Apostle   24
6 Joy Is Not Essentially a Feeling   26
7 Sorting Out the Meanings of "Joy"   28
8 The Joy of Christ's Cross   30
9 Doing God's Will   33
10 Heaven and Hell   35
11 The Two Things "God's Will" Means   38
12 Should We Pray for the Enjoyment of
   Earthly Things?   41
13 Joy Is a Cat, Not a Dog   44
14 Don't Get a "Spiritual Sweet Tooth"   46
15 Here Is the Infallible Argument for Joy   48
16 Isn't It Too Idealistic?   51
17 God or Joy? A Thought Experiment   54
18 Don't Give Up on Joy   56
19 What's the Catch?   59
20 Joy Is a Marriage   62
21 Real Joy versus Apparent Joy   64

22 Only Two Philosophies of Joy 67

23 How Joy Is Mystical 70

24 How Big Is Joy? 73

25 What of Agony? How Can That Be Joy? 75

26 Joy and Hope versus Entropy 77

27 The Roller Coaster 80

28 Evangelization through Joy 83

29 The Simplest Concrete Icon of Joy 85

30 Joy Is Ek-static 87

31 Joy Is the Water, and the Brain Is a Faucet
Handle 89

32 Taking Stock: What We Know and
What We Don't 92

33 Taking Stock: More of What We Know
and What We Don't 94

34 The Trinitarian Basis for Joy 96

35 Joy's Trinity 98

36 Joy's Place and Order among the Fruits
of the Spirit 100

37 Does God Enjoy Our Joys? 102

38 Three Levels of Reality and Joy 105

39 Why Isn't the Way to Joy Simple and Easy
to Find? 107

40 Why Does the Eucharist Give Us Joy? 109

41 What Happens in the Eucharist to Give Joy? 112

42 That's Great, but What If I Don't Feel the Joy? 114

43 Christ Is All "Four Causes" of Our Joy 116

44 The Mystery of Withness 118

45 What Does the Bible Say about Joy? 120

46 How Do We Offer Our "Prayers, Works,
   Joys, and Sufferings"?   121

47 The Basis for Our Joy Is the Nature of God   123

48 The Simplest Secret of Joy   125

49 The Joy of Purgatory and the Difference
   It Makes Now   127

50 Joy Is Visible   129

51 Living Purple or Living Beige   131

52 One More Time: Joy, Sorrow, Suffering,
   and Love   133

53 The Way to Joy Is and Is Not Rocket Science   135

54 Is It Selfish to Seek Our Own Joy?   137

55 Christ or Joy?   139

56 What Causes the Greatest Joy?   141

57 Why Is "How Do We Get This Joy?" a
   Trick Question?   143

58 Joy for Christ or Christ for Joy?   145

59 Joy's Eschatology   147

60 How *Sobornost* Magnifies Joy   149

61 How Does It All Work?   152

62 Joy in Old Age?   155

63 Is It Really God or Nothing? No Joy apart
   from God?   157

64 How Can We Have Joy in Heaven If Someone
   We Love Is in Hell?   159

65 Joy and Sorrow in the Rosary   162

66 Some of the Heavenly Appetizers of Joy
   and Glory   164

67 Does God Change His Love toward Us When
   We Change Ours toward Him?   166

68 Love Times *X* Equals Joy. What Is *X*? 168

69 Buddha's Salvation from Suffering—
and from Joy 171

70 Why Joy *Must* Conquer Sorrow 174

71 My Favorite Proof of Original Sin 177

72 From What Perspective Do We Look
at the World? 180

73 How Can Sorrows Be Turned into Joys? 182

74 City of Joy 185

75 The Stupidest Prize in the World 188

76 The Two Halves of Life 190

77 The Secret of the Joy of the Saints 192

78 Seven Obstacles to Joy 195

79 The Argument One More Time 197

80 God's Love as the Cause of Our Deepest Joy 199

81 God's Power as a Cause of Our Joy 201

82 The First Supernatural Bank and Trust
Company 203

83 Simplicity as a Cause of Our Joy 205

84 Hope and a Joyful Death 207

85 Charity as a Cause of Our Joy 210

86 The Communion of Saints as a Cause
of Our Joy 212

87 Mary as "Cause of Our Joy" 215

88 Angels as a Cause of Our Joy 218

89 Beauty as a Cause of Our Joy 220

90 Art as a Cause of Our Joy 223

91 Music as a Cause of Our Joy 226

92 Humor as a Cause of Our Joy 229

93 Seven Reasons Why Purgatory Is a Cause
    of Joy   232
94 The Real "Joy of Sex"   235
95 The Three Most Essential Sources of Joy   238
    Conclusion   239

INTRODUCTION

This introduction is mercifully short because if a book is any good at all, its introduction is the most boring part of it.

Let me dare to begin by being so perfectly honest with you about this book that you will probably throw it away. I am not a joy-full person. I am a Puddleglum and a pessimist. Happy people make me sad, especially happy pop psychologists and their disciples. I love curmudgeons like Samuel Johnson, Malcolm Muggeridge, Evelyn Waugh, J.R.R. Tolkien, and Murphy (of Murphy's Law). I can't stand "nice" people like Oprah and the nice, upbeat books she plugs. My concept of Purgatory is having to live with Ned Flanders of *The Simpsons*.

So what am I doing writing a book about joy? I'm *not* "sharing my feelings". I'm not writing about *my* joy. I'm writing about joy. I'm a philosopher, not a psychologist. I see more than I feel. (I also feel more than I see.)

I wrote a book entitled *Prayer for Beginners* even though I pray very poorly; and I wrote a book entitled *How to Be Holy* even though I'm a selfish sinner; and I wrote a book entitled *Wisdom of the Heart* even though my wisdom has worms and my heart has hemorrhoids. In other words, I'm saying "Do as I say, not as I do." It's a well-known paradox that comedians are usually *pagliacci*. Things, and especially people, are rarely what they seem to be. So maybe a curmudgeon can reveal some truths about joy that a happy face can't.

I'm writing this book to share with you not my *feelings* of joy but my *thoughts* about joy. And one of the most important and surprising of those thoughts is that joy is not essentially a feeling, just as love is not essentially a feeling.

A word about the book's design. The ideas about joy came to me one by one, in random order, and my first instinct was to put them down as they came, in random order, like Pascal's *Pensées*. But that seemed wrong. So I constructed a detailed outline, and that seemed wrong too—too logical, too academic. So I compromised. There is a general progression from joy to sorrow and, within joy, from its essence to its counterfeits and then to its properties and its causes and effects. The flow is not linear but in a kind of spiral, like a hunter circling a quarry. Thus, the main points are often repeated, because that's how our minds work and learn.

I also kept each of my ninety-five points, or pensées, short. I like short points, short chapters, and short books, and I suspect you do too. Our words, like our bodies, too often contain too much fat.

This book is not designed to be read straight through at one sitting, or a few, but to be read as you eat candies, only one or a few at a time.

I

The Need for This Book

The fact that you are reading this book proves you do not have the joy and peace that you want. If you were in Heaven now, you would not be reading a book about joy; you would be swimming in joy. Those who live in the golden castle do not read maps about how to get there.

The lack of deep joy has been true of all times, places, and cultures since Eden. But it is especially true of this time and this culture. No one writing about our culture would label it a "culture of joy". Our children still smile, but our young people do not, except at late-night dance clubs while fueled by drink and drugs. Africans who are poor still smile, and so do Mother Teresa's Missionaries of Charity. The poor smile more than the rich, and they commit suicide far less frequently. There is more prosperity *and* more suicide in Western civilization (which used to be called "Christendom") than anywhere else in the world. That is simply a fact.

Saint Thomas Aquinas writes that "no man can live without joy, and that is why a man deprived of spiritual joy goes over to carnal pleasures."[1] Substitutes become

---

[1] Thomas Aquinas, *Summa Theologica*, 1st complete American ed., vol. 2 of 3 (New York: Benziger Brothers, 1947), II-II, q. 35, art. 4, ad 2. Subsequent citations of *Summa Theologica* are from this edition. Hereafter cited as *ST*.

common when the real thing becomes rare. Did pornography exist in the past? Of course. Was it such a massive addiction as it is today? No.

We lack peace as well as joy. When I was a kid, we never heard of mass murderers shooting many strangers for no reason at all. It almost never happened. Maybe once a year. Now it happens every month!

Why? In Aleksandr Solzhenitsyn's scandalously simple words, "Men have forgotten God" (1983 Templeton Address). Muslims call that *ghaflah*. It's their version of Original Sin. That's why they pray five times a day. Do you?

Everything good begins with God, and the lack of everything good begins with the lack of God. If that is not true, then either there is no God or God is only *a* god, like Zeus.

We know true joy only through the true God; and we know the true God fully only through Jesus Christ, the complete revelation of God (Col 1:19); and we know Christ through the (usually anonymous) work of the Holy Spirit. The first three "fruits of the Spirit" are love, then joy, then peace, in that order (Gal 5:22). Love brings us joy, and joy brings us peace. Peace comes from joy, joy from love, love from the Spirit, the Spirit from the Son, and the Son from the Father. We lack peace today because we lack joy, and we lack joy because we lack love, and we lack love because we lack the Holy Spirit, for love is the first of His fruits. And the Spirit is sent by the Son, who is sent by the Father, the source of everything good. The three Persons are one God, whose whole life *is* love: unselfconscious, self-forgetful, self-giving, self-sacrificing *agape*. That is what God is. "God *is* love." To have love is to have God, and to have God is to have love (1 Jn 3:16; 4:8).

To live in that love, to *do* that love, is the secret of joy. And that joy is the secret of peace. It's that simple. But that simplicity is a rarity for our culture. A complex thing like your iPhone can't do it. Only you can.

How? It's scandalously simple. There's no method; you just do it. Methods are causes, and the effect can't be greater than the cause, but nothing greater exists that can cause love and its joy, since it is the very life of God. Let Him live in you and do it in you. Die to every other god, every idol. Be free of all your many addictions. Be "poor in spirit" (Mt 5:3); be detached from everything else, every psychological idol, and attached to the one true God, who *is* true joy.

.

2

What Is Joy?

Joy is to happiness what happiness is to pleasure: the next step up.

Sigmund Freud is famous for his "pleasure principle". He says we are all born innately longing for pleasure and hating pain. Obviously he is right there; but equally obviously he is wrong in saying that the "pleasure principle" dominates everything in us, including everything that is apparently greater.

Aristotle says that the thing we all seek, want, desire, long for, and are teleologically designed for is happiness. He meant by happiness (*eudaimonia*) not (1) a temporary (2) feeling (3) of contentment but (1) a lasting (2) and objectively real state (3) of goodness of soul or spirit (*eu-daimon-ia*).

(1) Because it was lasting, he said that it was a lifetime rather than a moment that constituted happiness. (2) Because it was not just a subjective feeling but an objectively real state of really perfecting our human nature, he said that it required work and suffering to perfect us, like a work of art. (3) And because it requires our moral and intellectual virtues (good habits) that perfect our human nature, he emphasized the need for the four cardinal virtues of wisdom, courage, self-control, and justice. He should have added mercy, honesty, kindness, and empathy for the same reason. None of

these virtues comes without suffering, and all of them are needed for real happiness.

But joy is even more than happiness. Unlike happiness, joy never gets boring because it is always a surprise. It is not mere contentment or satisfaction of our desires. It is not planned. It is a gift, a grace. Thus the title of C. S. Lewis' autobiography: *Surprised by Joy.*

Joy is a mystery. It is bigger than we are. Happiness is in us, but we are in joy. We enter into it; it does not enter into us.

Joy is self-forgetful. All the most joyful experiences you remember were self-forgetful. If you turned your eyes around from the thing that gave you the joy and looked at yourself, you lost the joy. Joy is "ek-static". (Literally, "ecstasy" means "standing outside yourself".) It is an out-of-your-mind experience as well as an out-of-the-body experience, because you do not think of your mind *or* your body when you are in joy. Because it is "ek-static" in this literal (and mystical) sense, it is ecstatic in the popular sense: greater than happiness, higher and deeper than mere contentment.

There are thus three levels of perfection in the heart's loves and desires: pleasure, happiness, and joy. There are similarly three levels in the intellect: sense perception (of facts), knowledge (of truth), and wisdom (understanding). In each case, the lowest level is shared with the animals (this does not make it bad or wrong or valueless, by any means), and the highest one is shared with God and the angels.

But joy is not just psychological and subjective. And that is the next point—a surprising one.

3

Joy Is Not in Us; We Are in Joy

Here is probably the most surprising idea in this book: that joy is not essentially a subjective feeling but an objective fact. We know we have joy by our faith, not by our feelings. When faith follows fact, it flourishes; when faith follows feeling, it falls.

Even what I have called the second or middle level, happiness (*eudaimonia* or *makarios*), is an objective state of blessedness. Thus, it can include suffering: "Blessed are those who mourn" (Mt 5:4). The pious poor often say how "blessed" they are, even for the little they have. The irreligious rich hardly ever use that word, even for their superabundant wealth. Only pleasure, the lowest level, is merely subjective: if you feel pleasure, you have it, and that's it.

Feelings are subjective: in us, dependent on us. They enter into us and exit out of us because they are smaller than we are. But true joy is bigger than we are because it is God Himself. We enter into it (Mt 25:21).

And since it is an objective fact rather than just a subjective feeling, we can have it even if we do not feel it. Christ *is* our joy, and we can have Christ always; therefore, we can have joy always. But we do not have the feeling of joy always. Therefore, joy is not merely the feeling of joy. That's unanswerable logic.

Ironically, it is a great comfort—and comfort is a feeling—to know that even when we do not feel it, Christ's joy is there! If we have Him, we have joy. The word "comfort" contains the syllable "fort", as in "fortitude" or as in an army "fort" or "fortress". It is a castle, not a kiss.

Christ is not merely the external cause of our joy, as Santa Claus is the cause of the Christmas presents under the tree; He is also the internal essence and identity of our joy. In Aristotelian terms, He is not merely the efficient cause of our joy but also the formal and material cause of our joy. He *is* our joy.

To see the difference between objective and subjective joy, imagine a perfect fake-joy machine that could give you the feeling of joy artificially, by manipulating your brain, without any objective reality as the reason and cause of your joy. Would you consent to live forever in the fake-joy machine if it freed you from all sorrow, suffering, frustration, fear, boredom, and death? Would you want to live in a cosmic Disneyland? Or would you prefer the real world, with its pains and pleasures, sorrows and joys, wars and peaces, hates and loves, betrayals and fidelities? Do you want to know and live in truth and reality, even if it entails feelings of sorrow and suffering, or do you want good feelings at the expense of truth and reality?

You may think that's a hard question to answer, but it isn't. What it really means is, Do you want to live in the world God willed for you or the one you desire for yourself? Do you want to live "Thy will be done" or "My will be done"? That question ultimately separates Heaven and Hell.

In Saint Augustine's sermon "On the Pure Love of God", he asks, If God offered you a deal in which you could have absolutely everything you desired except just one thing, the real God, would you take that "deal"? Or do you love God with your whole heart, above all else? Do you reply to God as Saint Thomas Aquinas did when God said to him, "You have written well of me, Thomas. What will you have as your reward?" His answer—the most perfect possible one—was three words: "Only Thyself, Lord." Is that your answer too?

4

C. S. Lewis' Mistake about Joy

C. S. Lewis was one of the most brilliant minds of modern times; yet even he succumbed for years to something like the mistake of subjectivizing joy. In his autobiography, *Surprised by Joy*, he defined "joy" in an unusual way: not as the satisfaction of a desire but as a desire: as his heart's deepest longing for something he could neither define (cf. 1 Cor 2:9) nor attain in this world. He called that desire itself "joy" because it was "more desirable than any other satisfaction."[1] He identified it with the German concept of *Sehnsucht*, the mysterious longing of the Romantic poets.

He was not wrong to put a higher value on that desire itself than on any other possible or conceivable satisfaction; and thus, he naturally craved to repeat the experience of that longing, that "restless heart". But he was wrong to think that what he was longing for was that experience itself. *That* "joy", he later discovered, was only a *sign* that pointed beyond itself. It had sign-ificance. It was like a pointing finger. But instead of following its pointing, Lewis for years fell in love with the finger. As the thirsty hart (deer) pants after the water brooks (Ps 42:1), so panted his heart for what he thought was joy but what really was God.

[1] C. S. Lewis, *Surprised by Joy: The Shape of My Early Life* (New York: Harper-One, 1955), 19.

The whole meaning and value of "joy" was not joy itself, just as the object of faith is not faith and the object of hope is not hope and the object of love is not love and the object of fear is not fear (as in FDR's "we have nothing to fear but fear itself") and the object of guilt is not guilt (as with some Freudian psychoanalysts who make us feel guilty about feeling guilty). The true object of this *Sehnsucht*, of this longing that Lewis called "joy", is not itself but God. Joy is only a reflection of Him and a signpost pointing to Him.

There was a profound truth at the heart of Lewis' mistake. Next to God Himself, the most precious and joyful thing in life is seeking Him, even if anonymously, as it was for the preconversion Lewis. Thus, the psalmist says, "Let the hearts of those who seek the LORD rejoice!" (Ps 105:3); and Lewis intuitively knew that it was right to "rejoice", i.e., to "take joy", in this seeking, because it is really seeking God, and thus it is the second-best thing in the world, next to finding God. This "natural hope" is the natural and instinctive substrate, or soil, for the supernatural "theological virtue" of hope, as instinctive trust is to faith and instinctive love is to charity.

As a Platonist, Lewis saw everything in this world as a sign, an image, of something beyond this world. Lions were images of kings, and kings were images of God's kingship. Lambs were images of sacrifice, and sacrifice was an image of God's self-sacrificial love. For Lewis, Plato's famous "Ideas" are not merely objects of the mind (universals, categories, kinds, forms, species, natures, or essences) but also objects of the will, the heart, and love. The "Big Idea" for Plato, after all, was not merely Truth but Goodness, which he saw in the *Symposium* as identical with Beauty. Truth, Goodness, and Beauty are one in God.

That "abomination of desolation" (Mt 24:15, KJV) called deconstructionism says that nothing has real significance, that nothing is a sign but simply a thing; that ideas are not labels but weapons in gender, race, and class wars. But Plato, Aquinas, and Lewis say that even things are signs, since they were designed by God, who wrote three books of signs that speak to us: nature, Scripture, and conscience (Rom 1:19–21).

Lewis shocks many readers when he confesses, on the very last page of his autobiography, that the subject of joy has lost almost all interest for him now that he is a Christian. When we are lost in the woods, a sign is terribly important, but not when we are on the path following that sign to Jerusalem.

5

The Last Commandment
of the Last Apostle

The practical takeaway for us from the previous point, about not mistaking the joy that is a sign of God for God Himself, is obedience to the last command of the last apostle: "Little children, keep yourselves from idols" (1 Jn 5:21).

Love, joy, peace, and the other fruits of the Spirit are great things, but they are not God Himself. And therefore, they can easily become idols. Satan's most effective idols are not little things (no one worships paper clips) but fake versions of great things. For instance, drugs mimic ecstatic out-of-body experiences, and lust mimics love, and joyless religion mimics joyful religion, and selfish pleasure mimics self-transcending joy. Satan can tempt us even with good and great things that are less than God if he can deceive us into adoring them instead of God: e.g., loving love, hoping in hope, having faith in faith, and taking joy in joy itself. These are all great gifts from God, but none of these is God Himself. As Muslims remind us, "Only God is God." God is not Santa Claus; His only present is Himself. He cannot give us anything better because there *is* nothing better. He does not *give* us joy; He *is* our joy.

Here is a great prayer, from William Cowper: "The dearest idol I have known, / Whate'er that idol be, / Help me to tear it from Thy throne / And worship only Thee."

Let not joy itself be that idol. God is our joy; joy is not our God.

Similarly, God is love, but love is not our God.

If love, joy, truth, goodness, beauty, faith, hope, and peace are not our God, what is our God?

Do we have to go to the Muslims to find out? Their central prayer, the *shahādah*, is "Only God is God": "*La ilaha illa Allah!*" "Allah" is simply the Arabic word for "God". Muslims learned who God is from the same source Christians did: His self-revelation to the Jews. The central prayer of Judaism is similar: "Hear, O Israel: The LORD our God is one LORD" (Deut 6:4).

What, then, is God? Two answers. The first is that God is simply more, infinitely more, than we can say about Him in words. That is the answer common to Jews, Christians, and Muslims. The second is the most basic reason for being a Christian: that Jesus Christ, the Word of God, is the definitive revelation of God in human form, "God from God, light from light, true God from true God", the only total and adequate answer to the question. "In him all the fulness of God was pleased to dwell" (Col 1:19).

He is the whole point of our faith, our hope, our love, our joy, and our peace.

6

Joy Is Not Essentially a Feeling

Like love, joy is not a feeling. Like love, joy is the very life of God.

People today are shocked to be told that love is also not essentially a feeling or an emotion but an act of the will. But this must be true, for love is a commandment—in fact, God's first and greatest commandment—and emotions cannot be commanded; only acts of the will and of free choice can. "I command you to feel positive feelings toward me"—that's simply nonsense, and God does not speak nonsense. Saint Thomas Aquinas defines love, simply and accurately (pretty much everything he says is said simply and accurately), as "willing the good of the other".[1] Love is goodwill.

Aquinas then goes on to say that there are two moments in love. When the good is absent, love takes the form of desiring that absent good. When the good is present, love takes the form of enjoying, joying-in, and affirming the present good.

Joy is this second form of love. Both love and joy are essentially acts of the free will, acts of choice, although they are usually also accompanied by feelings. Like love, joy spills out into the emotions most powerfully and helpfully. But they are its product, not its essence; its leaves,

[1] *ST* I-II, q. 26, art. 4 (vol. 1). All subsequent citations of *Summa Theologica* are from this volume.

not its root. The leaves of a plant come naturally and spon-
taneously; the root must be deliberately planted. That is
what we are responsible for, and that is what we will be
judged on. Saint John of the Cross says that "in the evening of our life we will be judged on our love" (*Dichos* 64).
The Last Judgment is not about feelings.

Here is a second and even better answer to the question,
If joy is not an emotion, what else could it be? The surprising answer is that it is a Person, a divine Person. Christ
is our joy.

One of the most shocking things Christ said was, "I am ...
the truth" (Jn 14:6). Truth is not merely something abstract,
such as an idea in us, or the correspondence between an idea
and a fact, or the relationship between a mind and reality,
but a Person. Similarly, joy is not essentially an emotion or
even an act of the will in us but is the life of God Himself
en-joying the good that is always present in Him. Just as
Christ, God Incarnate, is not merely a prophet or a teacher
of truth but the Truth itself, so He is not merely the external
efficient cause of our joy; He *is* our joy. Thus, even when
we do not feel joy, we have it if we have Him. Our feelings
are not infallible standards of reality!

It is almost impossible for the typically modern mind to
comprehend this because it is almost impossible for that
mind to detach itself from feelings. Feelings are divine gifts
and are proper and natural, but today they function like
a spider's web and we are like the flies imprisoned and
suffocated by it. Thus, we often see not only joy but even
faith, hope, and love as feelings. But God is not such a bad
psychologist as to command us to do what is not under our
free will or control. Joy, love, faith, and hope are indeed
under our free will, but feelings are not; therefore, they are
not feelings. They are much more than that, but they are not
less than that.

7

Sorting Out the Meanings of "Joy"

At this point, you are probably confused because there are at least four meanings of the word "joy": (1) the ordinary sense, as a feeling or emotion similar to but deeper than happiness, (2) C. S. Lewis' sense of a *longing* for joy in some object that is unattainable and indefinable in this life (which Lewis later discovered was God), (3) the act of will by which we en-joy a present good, and (4) the infallible promise given to us by Christ that He Himself *is* our joy.

Let's begin with an interior map. We are body and soul, and within the soul we have three powers that animals do not have: reason, or intellectual understanding; rational will, or free will, or free choice; and spiritual feelings or emotions. Mere animal emotions, nonspiritual or nonrational emotions, include just feeling OK or not OK for no apparent reason; contentment; a vague, apparently meaningless discontent; fear of pain; desire for pleasure; hating present pain; and enjoying present pleasure. Spiritual, rational (in the broad, ancient sense), or distinctively human emotions include wonder, gratitude, compassion, trust, awe, guilt, hate, and desire for revenge. One meaning of "joy" is the distinctly human emotion that is to happiness what happiness is to pleasure: another, deeper dimension.

Lewis uses the word in a second sense: as a *desire* rather than an enjoyment—a desire for what he at first thought was simply a deeper experience of joy but later came to realize was, in fact, nothing less than God. This Lewisian "joy" is Augustine's "restless heart", which cannot rest in anything less than God (Saint Augustine, *Confessions* 1, 1).

A third sense would be the act of affirming, or enjoying, any present good, especially the greatest good in this life—namely, the incomplete joy of en-joying God's real presence and love. In Heaven this will be a much more complete but still finite union of wills and minds (the "Beatific Vision") with the infinite Being who is the source and giver of all joy. (This third sense is close to the theological virtue of hope.)

A fourth sense of "joy", found in Scripture, is the assurance of God's reality, presence, and providential love. This fourth sense is, in fact, the very life of God in our souls, a finite spark of the fire of the infinite joy of God Himself.

If these distinctions have added to your confusion rather than subtracted from it, I beg your forgiveness and advise you just to plunge into the rich jungle of joy that the rest of this book explores without a totally clear road map. The jungle without the map is much better than the map without the jungle.

8

The Joy of Christ's Cross

Our joy includes a cross. Christ asks us to share His cross with him, like Simon of Cyrene—actually to share His act of carrying it. This is not mere imitation but a real participation in His act. "Participation" in it means becoming a part of it, becoming literally in-corporated, in-bodied into it. For we are not just His imitators or followers; we are His (Mystical) Body.

What moved Him to carry His cross, then, must also move us. What was it? Joy! "Jesus ... for the joy that was set before him endured the cross, despising [ignoring] the shame" (Heb 12:2). What was that "joy that was set before him"? His future relief from the cross could not be His motive for enduring it; that would be like hitting yourself with a hammer for the sake of feeling joyful relief when you stopped. "Before" sometimes means the past, as yesterday is "before today", but here it means the present, as a meal is "presented" or set "before" us in the *present* time, to be eaten in the present or at least in the immediate future, which is part of what we usually mean by the "present".

So that joy was not merely the joys that He knew would come afterward in Heaven and how much they would outweigh the sufferings. Saint Teresa of Avila said that the most terrible life on earth, when we look back on it from the perspective of Heaven, will seem no more serious than one night in an inconvenient hotel. So what joy did Christ have in the present that was set before Him when He was enduring the cross?

The joy Christ had in His terrible Passion was the certain and infallible knowledge that His deeds were saving those He loved from Hell and opening to them the joys of Heaven. The more you love someone, the more joy you have in saving him. Even if that "saving" is painful, it is at the same time a joy.

It was also the joy of doing what was His supreme good and should also be our supreme good: the will of God. That was what He said He came into this world for: "I seek not my own will but the will of him who sent me" (Jn 5:30).

And this joy in suffering is possible for us too, however imperfectly, at least as an ingredient in our sufferings and sorrows, our mixed motives, like the few drops of wine an Italian parent mixes in a glass of water for his very young children at supper, as a tiny taste of a vastly different thing. After all, Jesus is not only perfect God but also perfect man, our model and standard and pioneer. He suffered in His human nature (not His divine nature, which cannot suffer), so we cannot say, "It was easy for Him because He was God, but we are not." He was also man, and we are too.

Even if Jesus *felt* no joy in His Passion, He *willed* it; He "*took* joy" in it because He *knew* that He was obeying the Father and saving man. And we can know that too: we can know that we are suffering *from* God's will and *for* God's will, which is His children's salvation. We are His co-operators, His dependent co-redeemers. And the more we love God and His children, the more we, too, can take joy in this holy and heavenly work. Compared with that, feelings are almost trivial.

In Purgatory we will understand this by experience. Our will will be freed from sin and rebellion and will be completely aligned with God's will, so that we will *will* our sufferings. Therefore, they will be great joys as well as great sufferings.

9

Doing God's Will

Jesus said that He came to do the will of the Father.

He did not say that He came to take away all our sufferings and sorrows.

He did not say that He came to make us happy, comfortable, or content.

He did not say that He came to make us wise rabbis and teachers.

He did not say that He came to give us mystical experiences.

He did not say that He came to teach us a new morality. There is no such thing as a new morality, any more than there is a new multiplication table.

He did not say that He came for power and triumph and glory.

He said that He came because the Father sent Him.

He came and suffered and died for us because He obeyed His Father's will and because He loved us. Those are to be our two absolutes, our two Great Commandments, as they were His.

When you know you are doing God's will, you forget everything else, even joy.

And then you get joy.

In fact, when you forget everything else, you get everything else.

If we seek first the Kingdom of God and His righteousness, all else will be added (Mt 6:33).

If we seek first our own kingdom, all will be subtracted.

Heaven and Hell

If you had to choose between a perfect Heaven and complete joy without God, or God without a perfect Heaven and complete joy, which would you choose?

There is a great Jim Carrey movie that touches on that choice. It is *The Truman Show*, in which Carrey lives in an artificial Utopian community that is an enormous TV prop, a cosmic Disneyland. It's perfect—too perfect. As that great philosopher Yogi Berra said, "If the world were perfect, it wouldn't be."

There was a *Twilight Zone* episode in which an evil criminal apparently went to Heaven and got whatever he wanted: gold, girls, glitz, whatever. But he was not happy. He asked the Saint Peter figure, "Isn't everybody supposed to be happy in Heaven? Why ain't I happy?" And the answer was, "Why do you ask about Heaven? Heaven is the Other Place."

C. S. Lewis wrote in *The Problem of Pain*, "As there may be pleasures in hell (God shield us from them), there may be something not all unlike pains in heaven (God grant us soon to taste them)."[1] The essence of Hell is not pain, and the essence of Heaven is not pleasure. The difference

---

[1] C. S. Lewis, *The Problem of Pain* (New York: HarperOne, 1940), 157.

between Heaven and Hell is not the difference between pleasure and pain.

What is it then? Lewis answered that question in *The Great Divorce*, his Dantean masterpiece about Heaven and Hell: "There are only two kinds of people in the end: those who say to God, 'Thy will be done,' and those to whom God says, in the end, '*Thy* will be done.'"[2] The lyrics everyone sings in Hell is Frank Sinatra's "I did it my way." The lyrics everyone sings in Heaven is "God's way is the best way" (1911 hymn by Lida Shivers Leech). What does that have to do with joy? The point is that the essence of joy is "Thy will be done", not "My will be done." The power that makes joy, as bees make honey, is not the feelings but the will.

Heaven is where God's will is done. There are two places that fit that description: the place where God and the blessed live eternally after death, and the lives of God's children here on earth. That's why Saint Teresa of Avila reputedly said that "all the way to Heaven is Heaven."

"All the way to Heaven" is also Purgatory, for Purgatory is the first part of Heaven for most of us. It is Heaven's bathroom, where we wash before dinner. All of life is Purgatory. Its divine design, both before and after death, is meant to change us from selfish and (therefore) sorrowful sinners to self-giving and (therefore) joyful saints—i.e., from "My will be done" to "Thy will be done" in all things, 100 percent. All the events of our lives are "meant" to do that, for that is "the 'meaning' of life", to become saints. (That is also a proof for the existence of God, for a "meaning" is "meant" only by a Mind. A "meaning" does not just "happen" like a rainstorm.)

When we die, if this life of grace is not in us at all, we cannot enter Heaven. If it is in us completely (100 percent),

[2] C. S. Lewis, *The Great Divorce* (New York: HarperOne, 1946), 75.

we go straight to Heaven. If it is in us only partially, we go to Purgatory first. The more our desires and desiring habits are sinful (and therefore sorrowful), the more Purgatory we need in order to enjoy and endure heavenly joy. This world is God's workshop, where He providentially sculpts our souls. That is why Purgatory is joyful as well as painful, like childbirth.

The Two Things
"God's Will" Means

Theologians often distinguish between God's revealed will and God's secret will, or God's commanding will and God's permissive will, or God's direct will and God's indirect will. God does not have two wills, but His single will appears to us, and impacts our lives, in two ways. He commands faith, hope, love, and all the moral virtues; He permits failures, sorrows, sufferings, and even sins (though, of course, He does not approve of them or love them), all for the sake of our greater good in the end (Rom 8:28).

God's *commanding* will commands only good things, good choices, good actions, and good motives. He does not command sins or sufferings. Our response to God's commanding will is to be obedient, in love and faith and trust and hope. God's *permissive* will allows sufferings into our lives for the sake of our greater joy in the end (why else would God permit them?) and also our greater sanctity (for we cannot become saints without suffering). He also permits us to sin by giving us free will in the first place and then by often withholding graces that could prevent us from sinning, in order to prevent worse sins, especially pride. If He appeared to us now in all His glory and beauty, as He will appear in Heaven in the Beatific

Vision, we would become incapable of sinning or even being tempted. But He does not. Why? For the same reason good parents don't do their children's homework for them.

Sometimes the reason may be not our own greater good in the end but that of others. We exist not just for ourselves but also for others, as others exist not just for themselves but also for us.

Willing God's commanding will means obedience. Willing God's permissive will means trust—trust that God knows better than we do what is best for us. That's hard emotionally, but it's easy intellectually: Can we really think we are wiser than God?

We get joy from both willings, from both obedience and trust. As the old hymn says, somewhat sentimentally and simplistically, "Trust and obey, for there's no other way to be happy in Jesus but to trust and obey" (1887 hymn by Reverend J. H. Sammis).

The two right reactions to the two ways God's twofold will comes to us are different. The first right reaction, obedience, is in response to God's revealed will, or commandments. It is an act or action or activity. The second reaction, to God's permissive will, is an acceptance, a receptivity, a trust and surrender or submission (an "islam"), motivated by faith and hope and love. Both this activity and this acceptance give us joy, as we can see from the connection between the two meanings of the word "islam"—namely, "surrender" and "peace". "Islam" ("surrender") and "shalom" ("peace") have the same root, the consonants s-l-m. T. S. Eliot said that the greatest line in all of merely human literature is Dante's "In His will, our peace."[1]

[1] Dante, *Paradiso* 3, 85.

God does not have two wills. The two wills are really one because God's revealed will is part of His secret will, since *everything* is part of His secret will, what Aquinas calls "the eternal law" in the Mind of God.[2]

[2] *ST* I-II, q. 93, art. 2.

Should We Pray for the Enjoyment of Earthly Things?

God is love, and love wills the good of the beloved, so God wills our good, temporal as well as eternal. Our temporal good includes earthly things, such as good health, good food, good art, and good feelings; and since these are good, it is obviously right for us to enjoy them, to take joy in them when they are present and to desire them when they are absent. And when they are absent, we should obviously pray for these things in our petitionary prayers, as well as the much more important things that prepare us for Heaven—namely, faith, hope, and charity. We should pray to God to relieve us of both our physical and our spiritual poverty.

The question is whether we should pray with the assurance that we will get these earthly things we pray for. We know that God always wills our faith, hope, and charity to increase, but we also know that God does not always will that our health or food or art or wealth increases. So when we pray to get these earthly joys, such as recovery from disease, should we have faith that God will grant our petition on earth? If we had enough faith, would we be able to move earthly mountains as well as spiritual ones? Is it a lack of faith or of our personal intimacy with and knowledge of

God, or both, that would lead us to pray only "Thy will be done, whatever it is" rather than "I know You will give me this earthly good"?

Should we always be detached from earthly goods and seek God alone? When Mary implicitly asked Christ for the earthly good of more wine at the wedding feast at Cana, her intimate knowledge of Him and trust in Him were rewarded. But when Christ asked His Father, "If it be possible, let this chalice [of suffering, the Crucifixion] pass from me", He added, "nevertheless, not as I will, but as you will" (Mt 26:39). Which pattern are we to follow?

The answer has to be both, somehow. What they have in common is the faith that God will always give us what is best in the end, even though it seemingly deprives us of joy now. It seems that some believers (and not merely the great saints) are sometimes given by God the assurance that He will give them the things asked for here on earth, in time, visibly and literally; but it also seems that some (apparently most) are not given this assurance. So it is not our lack of faith that makes us hesitate to "name it and claim it" concretely (e.g., recovery from disease, injustice, poverty, even psychological problems, such as clinical depression). It is simply the honesty to confess that we do not, at least now, know God so intimately and personally that we are in on His hidden providential plans. And that is the much more common situation, even for the saints.

The distinction between joy as an emotion and joy as an act of the will is also needed here. We are always to pray for joy as an act of the will, for that is a moral virtue. Not to enjoy a present good is almost as evil as not to desire an absent good. We know that God always wills that joy. But God does not always will that we have the *feelings* of joy; He often wills (permits) sufferings for us. But we should, and therefore can, pray "Thy will be done" then too, because we trust His wisdom to know, as we do not, that that suffering is best for us in the end. We should resist the temptation to "play God" and pretend we know more than we know. That is a sin against honesty and humility, both of which are extremely important virtues. The "name it and claim it" "prosperity gospel" is a harmful heresy.

13

Joy Is a Cat, Not a Dog

Dogs come when called. Cats come when they please. Dogs come under the category of what Niccolò Machiavelli calls our *virtu*, or power: what we can control. Cats come under the category of what he calls *fortuna*, or chance: what we cannot control. (His formula for success was simply to maximize *virtu* and minimize *fortuna*. In other words, to play God, not to trust God. He was a functional atheist.)

Joy comes like a cat, not a dog, because it does not come when we whistle. It comes not at our will but at its own will—which is really ultimately God's will, for God's providence extends to both cats and dogs.

There are other things that are catlike in that way: pleasure, happiness, humor, and health are four of them.

Pleasure is the greatest when it is a surprise, when it is not under our control.

The same for happiness. People make themselves more unhappy by deliberately seeking happiness and fearing unhappiness. Hypochondriacs worry themselves sick about getting sick and obsess about health; and happiness hypochondriacs worry themselves unhappy about being unhappy and obsess about happiness.

The same is true of humor. It can't be controlled. In fact, the punch line of every good joke is always something unexpected and uncontrolled, like laughter itself, when the body shares the soul's ecstasy.

Let joy come, at God's will. Let God do His thing; it's better than your thing because He's a better God than you could be. If you don't believe that, watch the movie *Bruce Almighty*.

14

Don't Get a "Spiritual Sweet Tooth"

All the saints say not to crave "sensible consolations". "Sensible" here means neither "perceptible to the five senses" nor "reasonable or commonsensical" but "emotional"; "sensible consolations" refer to what we today usually mean by "experiences". "Sensible consolations" are like sugar. God does not give us as much as we would like because He knows it is harmful to us to get a spiritual "sweet tooth", an addiction to the sugar. Sensible consolations, including the subjective experience of joy, are not the soul's food, only the taste of the food. The food is *agape* love, the adoration of God, the obedience to God's will ("If you love me, you will keep my commandments" [Jn 14:15]), and charity to our neighbors.

The saints surprise us in many ways. One of them is that they all say emotions are far less important than we think. Our life's task is to become saints, not to become bubbles of joy. Saints have true joy, but true joy is not bubbly. Bubbles are usually on the surface, fragile and poppable.

Another thing the saints say that surprises us is that methods of prayer and sanctification, though not wrong and sometimes helpful, are also far less important than we think. Methods, for doing anything, are always ways of controlling effects, a kind of technology. Physical technology compels matter to behave according to our will, but there is no such thing as spiritual technology. Methods cannot cause sanctity or joy because the effect cannot be greater than the cause, and there is nothing greater than sanctity, which is the life of God. That is why there can be no "holiness machine".

What, then, can we do to find joy, if there is no machine or technology or technique that can infallibly cause it? Only God can give it; we can only ask for it. But we ask not only by asking but also by loving. The secret of joy is to love God and what God omnisciently, omni-benevolently, and omnipotently wills for us—not what we witlessly, wickedly, and weakly will for ourselves—as well as to love our spiritual siblings, our "neighbors", as God loves them.

But you knew that already. Are you disappointed not to find a new, hidden, "occult" method for joy? Stop looking for something new. This is not science and technology; this is common sense and tradition, divine revelation already given in conscience and in Scripture. The only way to our Omega is to return to our Alpha.

15

Here Is the Infallible Argument
for Joy

Either God exists, or He does not. What I mean here by
"God" is the minimal definition of the word: a being who
is not weak, witless, or wicked, like all the gods of polythe-
ism. To deserve the name "God", God must have unlimited power, knowledge, and goodness. John the Evangelist
calls these "life" (*zoe*), "light" (*phos*), and "love" (*agape*);
Hinduism calls them Brahman's *sat* (infinite being, power,
or life), *chit* (infinite knowledge, wisdom, or understanding), and *ananda* (infinite joy, from infinite goodness and
love). These are the three things that all of us need and
want, and not just in limited but in unlimited quantity.

If God does not exist, then these three things do not
exist in infinite quantities, only in their finite, imperfect
forms as they exist in us. In fact, if God does not exist, they
are merely our subjective wishes, not objective realities.
They have no home in Being, only in our dreaming. If
there is no God, there can be no image of God in man, no
immortal spirit; death always will have the last word, and
the sign over the door to Hell that reads "Abandon hope,
all ye who enter here"[1] ought to be put over the door to
earth—namely, the womb.

[1] Dante, *Inferno*, canto 3.

Bertrand Russell draws the unavoidably logical corollaries of atheism in these words:

> That Man is the product of causes which had no prevision of the end they were achieving; that his origin, his growth, his hopes and fears, his loves and his beliefs, are but the outcomes of accidental collocations of atoms; that no fire, no heroism, no intensity of thought and feeling, can preserve an individual life beyond the grave; that all the labours of the ages, all the devotion, all the inspiration, all the noonday brightness of human genius, are destined to extinction in the vast death of the solar system, and that the whole temple of Man's achievement must inevitably be buried beneath the debris of a universe in ruins—all these things, if not quite beyond dispute, are yet so nearly certain, that no philosophy which rejects them can hope to stand. Only within the scaffolding of these truths, only on the firm foundation of unyielding despair, can the soul's habitation henceforth be safely built.[2]

If God does not exist, that is the way things are. If God does exist, that is not the way things are. And if God (omnibenevolence, omniscience, and omnipotence) exists, His omnibenevolence wills only good for us, and His omniscience knows what is always best for us, and His omnipotence gets whatever He knows and wills. What logically and necessarily follows from these three obvious premises is the least obvious truth claim in the Bible, the one that requires the most faith yet the one that is the most irrefutably and necessarily true if these three nonnegotiable premises of theism are true. The verse is Romans 8:28, that "all things work together for good to them that love God, to them who are the called according to his purpose" (KJV).

---

[2] Bertrand Russell, "A Free Man's Worship", December 1903.

All who choose to swim in the river of God's will end up in the ocean of His joy.

This is our redoubt, our bastion, our castle keep, our pavilion, our fortress. "A mighty fortress is our God, a bulwark never failing." No one and nothing can defeat God's unlimited power, wisdom, and love. This is "the greatest story ever told", the goodest Good News, the thing all sane and good people most wish is true, and the irrefutable reason for joy. It is also the reason why "Thy will be done" is the best prayer, both objectively and subjectively, as the irrefutable objective reason for the subjective hope for eternal, unlimited, unimaginable, inconceivable, ecstatic joy. It's God or nothing.

16

Isn't It Too Idealistic?

How is this philosophy livable? Isn't it too good to be true? Can it be lived in the middle of this mysterious mess that is our earthly life? Life can be a terrible mess—a physical pain that cannot be relieved, or a personal betrayal, or the death of a child. Or it can even be a minor mess—a hemorrhoid, a fight with a friend, the death of a pet. These things don't all seem to work for the greater good. But Romans 8:28 must apply to these things as much as to everything else, for God is the God of everything.

If we saw everything working together for our greater good, we would need no faith, only sight, to pray, "Thy will be done." Our will and faith would not be tested. But faith is the heart of our lifeline to God. What would life be without faith? Godless and, therefore, in the deepest sense, joyless.

What is faith? It is not just thinking, a mental *opinion*. Nor is it a feeling. It is a free choice of the will. It is aided by good reasons, and it is helped or harmed by feelings. But, like hope and love, it is not essentially either a thought or a feeling but a choice, a responsibility, and a requirement for salvation.

Because they are free choices, faith and hope and love are always possible. They are often difficult, because our contrary feelings are many and strong. We are tempted to pride by feelings of success and to despair by feelings of frustration; to pride by feelings of contentment and to despair by feelings of failure. But even a weak but honest faith, smaller than a grain of mustard seed, is precious to God our Father, as a toddler's crude drawings are precious to his parents. And God will grow our faith: when we give Him an inch, He will take a mile. When we give Him a tiny burning ember of faith, He will blow it up into a bonfire.

So we can always say the words of faith and trust, "Thy will be done", in both of the senses distinguished earlier (see pensée 11): the "obey" sense to His commandments and the "trust" sense to His providence. For trust is also essentially an act of free will. We *choose* to "en-trust" everything to God as we choose to entrust our money to a bank. We cannot always feel or understand, but we can always choose. We can say thank you to God for all His gifts, even His gifts of pain, because we know, by faith, that everything is His gift—if not directly, as a good, then indirectly, as an evil that He allows only for our greater good. (He has no other reason to allow it if He is omnibenevolent!) Most things are good in the first sense, like foods. Sufferings are good in the second sense, like bitter but necessary medicines. If they were not necessary, our loving heavenly Father would not give them to us (cf. Lk 11:11–13).

This is easy to understand but difficult to live, because our faith and our reason are both weak compared with our feelings. But it is always justified, for it is always true. And it always increases our joy when it is done, even when obedience demands sacrifice and when trust demands endurance. Christ came not to take away our sufferings but to transform them into instruments of our salvation.

And also the salvation of others: every good we do helps not only our own salvation and sanctification and joy but also that of others in unseen ways, as their good helps us. And all our evils harm others; there are no victimless crimes. It is a kind of universal spiritual gravity that the Russians call *sobornost*. Would you rather be all alone and *not* be able to help and be helped by others toward salvation in that mysterious way?

17

God or Joy? A Thought Experiment

God is joy, both in Himself eternally and for us in time. But suppose we had to choose between God and joy? Suppose God said to us, "I will give you all joys except one: myself." (That was Augustine's "thought experiment" in his sermon "On the Pure Love of God".) Would we take that "deal"?

If we have faith, our answer is no. At least, that is the thing we would *want* to say to Him: "No, no, a thousand times no; stay with me, Lord, even if You lay a terrible cross on me. You are my Father, not my Santa Claus. Even if You have no presents for me, You are my present, my joy. Stay with me always." That is the point Augustine was making in that sermon.

Even an atheist, who cannot have that conversation with God, still can and should resist the temptation to enter an artificial "happiness machine" that would give him nothing but felt joys and no kinds of suffering, forever, simply because it is not real, not true. How much of modern technology constitutes our attempt to build that "happiness machine" in this world? And how has it worked? How happy are we today?

But pain strikes us more sharply than pleasure, sufferings more sharply than joys. Suppose the thought experiment was not about joys but about sufferings; not about choosing either all other joys without God or God's joy alone, but about sorrows and sufferings. Suppose our choice was between God plus terrible sufferings and the removal of both God and the sufferings. Suppose God appeared to us not with a crown but with a cross, at least for now. We would want to make the same choice, but it would be much harder.

But that is no thought experiment. That is real life. As soon as we exit the womb, we feel terror, "the primal scream". We have no other, Utopian option, no life without the ever-present possibility of pain, even terrible pain. So the question is really, Do we want to be born, or do we want to remain alone in the womb?

Plotinus, in his *Enneads*, said that heavenly "enlightenment" was "alone into the Alone" (6, 6), and Jean-Paul Sartre, in his *No Exit*, said that "Hell is other people." I know of no more totally false ideas about Heaven and Hell than those two. I suspect that Hell is pure aloneness, the total absence of all others, including God.

God is joy, but joy is not God. Similarly, God is love, but love is not God. God is our joy, but even if He were not our joy, God is God. Joy, you are not my God; God, you are my God. And You are also my joy.

18

Don't Give Up on Joy

So that last point is this: Don't idolize joy. But don't give up on it either. Don't be a stiff-upper-lip, clenched-teeth, duty-mongering Stoic. Duty and responsibility and obligation and obedience and loyalty are absolutely necessary but are not sufficient—not without joy, which comes from love. The object of duty is a principle, but the object of love is a person. We do not admire parents who do not love their children or each other but act only out of duty. Duty is only a second best, a fallback, the second line of battle, when love fails. (And it often does, temporarily, so duty is necessary.) When love fails, joy fails, for there is always some joy in love, however great the difficulties and sufferings.

Joyless Christians make no converts. Joyful ones do. The hard-nosed, practical Romans were much more impressed by the joy they saw in Christians than by their ideas and ideals and beliefs, which often seemed to make no sense to the Romans. But they saw that Christians were the only ones who risked their lives to minister to plague victims and smiled as they did it. They forgave their enemies and sang hymns as they were eaten by lions. That's data, not just ideas. As an old saying goes, "Who you are speaks so loud I can hardly hear what you say." Who we are as Christians is a more unanswerable argument than anything we say. That's true, and powerful, even if what we are is far, far less than saints.

It's true that doing a task or accepting a suffering that seems joyless is very hard. But there is a great joy even there, in the very act of obedience and the conquest of selfishness and the knowledge that we do God's will. Christ promised us, "My yoke is easy, and my burden is light" (Mt 11:30)—this from the One who knew He was about to be crucified!

Where was the joy there, spoken of in Hebrews 12:2, "the joy that was set before" Jesus, for which He "endured the cross"? First, it was knowing that this was God's will. That was the primary source of His joy, and it can and should be the primary source of ours.

Second, it was His love of us that gave Him joy because He knew that He, the Lamb of God, would take away the sins of the world. "The world" is not the world's political systems and structures but *us*, whom He loved with His whole divine heart. In that Great Exchange, He would take away the punishment we deserved and give us the reward that He deserved.

Third, doing hard things out of love for God and neighbor adds a kind of joy even within the act of suffering. Freely willing it turns it into an act instead of a victimization, as it did for Christ (Jn 10:18). This sometimes even mitigates the suffering. Carrying Frodo up Mount Doom, Sam, though exhausted, found the burden light. Perhaps Simon of Cyrene found Christ's cross light too.

Fourth, the divinely promised "payoff" (and our hope and anticipation of it) is enormous and eternal. It is more than the satisfaction of having done our duty; it is *glory*, both ours and God's. And that "sure and certain hope of the resurrection" (the carefully chosen words of the Catholic burial liturgy), and the assurance that Christ always keeps His promises, casts its bright shadow back onto our present otherwise-joyless task and fills it with glory, as childbirth does to labor pains and as Heaven does to earth.

19

What's the Catch?

The Devil walks into a lawyer's office. The lawyer asks politely, "What can I do for you, sir?" The Devil replies, "No, it's what I can do for you. I can make you incredibly rich and famous. All you have to do is sign this little contract of mine, giving me rights to your eternal soul, and those of your whole family, forever." The lawyer narrows his eyes suspiciously, takes the contract, carefully reads every line of it, and asks the Devil, "So what's the catch?"

All this stuff about joy even in suffering—it's a con job, a scam, a lie, a dream, right? That's why it's blind faith and not testable science, right? Wrong. It's testable in the laboratory of life. It has been proven over and over. You can repeat the experiment and prove it to yourself. (I call it an experiment because that is what it has to be for those who lack faith.) You will not be cheated, conned, or scammed. No one who has ever said to God and honestly meant, in his heart, "I trust You; Your will be done" has ever failed to find joy, even in that very act, not only in a remote future "payoff". "In His will, our peace."[1]

This joy and its peace are very similar to a woman's freely willed sexual surrender to a man, as many mystics and Doctors of the Church have taught. That's one reason

[1] Dante, *Paradiso* 3, 85.

"God" pronouns are always male even though God has no biological gender: because to Him all souls are female. It's analogy, not biology. It's not "sexist" privilege, for the same is true for a man as it is for a woman: he, too, must freely surrender to God's love initiative, must overcome the fear that demands control, and only thus find life's deepest joy. "Control freaks" fear the joy of surrender. Spiritual frigidity, like sexual frigidity, comes from fear; and fear is the passive side of egotism, as lust and greed are the active side. We all know people who are cold, suspicious, mistrustful, and unwilling to let go; and we see how wretched and joyless they are.

It's a logical order that's almost an equation: you need faith and trust in order to let go and love, and you need that love in order to have joy. Love is the fruit of faith, and joy is the fruit of love. If A, then B, and if B, then C; therefore, if A, then C.

This sounds suspiciously like a salesman's pitch. So what's the catch? There is a catch, and a big one. But it's a simple one: you really have to do it, not just think about it. And that requires dying. Not physically. The body is not the problem. The ego and self-will are the problem. That's what Saint Paul calls "the old man" or "the flesh"—fallen, sinful human nature (soul as well as body). This is distinct from "the new man" or "the spirit"—the self (body as well as soul) who has accepted the Holy Spirit, the Spirit of Christ, and has *zoe*, or supernatural life, the very life of God, not just *bios*, natural life. This natural life is "the old man" who has been conned by the Devil, who whispers to us as he whispered to our first parents, "Beware of God. He's a killer." Our "flesh" with its fallen, fearful, mistrusting, "what's the catch?" ego is his microphone.

There is always a twisted half-truth in what the Devil says. God *does* want to kill our selfish, joyless ego, but only out of love for us and our joy. He is a gentleman. He will seduce us, but He will not force us.

This is why sex is both so holy and so powerful: it is an image of the spiritual marriage between Christ and His Church, His Bride—us!—to be consummated in the New Jerusalem (Rev 19:7, 9; 21:2). And that is nothing less than the whole "meaning of life" and ultimate joy. For Heaven's sake, say yes to His marriage proposal!

20

Joy Is a Marriage

The attainment of joy, and of the other fruits of the Spirit—love, peace, patience—is not a do-it-yourself operation. It is a two-person operation, a marriage. You can't do it without God, and He won't do it without you, without your cooperation. ("Co-operation" means "with work".)

Actually, it is a three-person operation, because it requires not just a "me and God" relationship but equally a "me and others" relationship. It is like a marriage, in which the two become one, and there is a third. It is like the Trinity, in which the Spirit eternally proceeds from the love union between God the Father and God the Son. Marriage is the primary image of the Trinity. As Fulton Sheen put it in the title of the best book I know about the meaning of marriage, it takes *Three to Get Married*.

Dante's sign over Hell's door reads, "Abandon hope, all ye who enter here."[1] In Hell, there is no Other; that is why there is no hope. The worst Hell is not fire but absolute aloneness, the ego without an Other. For joy requires the ecstasy of standing outside ourselves, and the self itself cannot bring the self out of itself. How could it? The effect (joy) cannot be greater than the cause (the self, the ego, fallen human nature, man in Original Sin). How could

[1] Dante, *Inferno*, canto 3.

man-without-God change himself into man-with-God? God-without-man has the power to become God-with-man, but man-without-God does not have the power to become man-with-God.

If Nirvana exists, and if and when Buddhists attain Nirvana (which Buddha described as timeless "bliss" and "joy"), it is not for the reason they think—namely, human effort; it is because God's grace did it, although He remained anonymous. Shinran's "Pure Land" sect of Buddhism, which believes in "Other-power", is right about that; and other Buddhists, who go by Buddha's command to "be lamps unto yourselves", are simply wrong. Fortunately, God's mercy does not demand passing a theology test as a requirement for salvation, at least not in this life, although it may well be a requirement for graduation from Purgatory.

The geometrical sign for the most horrible torture ever devised is a cross. The geometrical sign for transcendence, or moreness, is also a cross: a plus sign, the sign for yes. It can be interpreted as a spiritual icon, for it takes the vertical bar, the I—the simple, lonely, joyless ego—and crosses it, crosses it out, contradicts it; but what emerges in the plus sign is another *dimension*, width as well as height, others as well as self. It is not a loss but a gain, not a death but a resurrection. Thus, to live truly, we must first die to ourselves. Even Buddha knew that.

21

Real Joy versus Apparent Joy

The distinction between appearance and reality is distinctively human and the origin of all philosophy and science. Questioning is a distinctively human enterprise. We do not just experience questions as we experience storms or trees; we create questions, since we know that appearances and reality are not identical, that appearances can deceive.

There are two kinds of deceiving appearances: external, sensory appearances (such as mirages and holograms) and internal, emotional appearances (such as the attractiveness of an indulged lust or the unattractiveness of a God-required difficult duty). Feelings are one kind of appearance: what is felt and what is real are not the same. Insofar as joy is a feeling, there are real, true joys and false, apparent joys.

The joys that come from our sins are false joys, like drugs or poisons. The appearance does not fulfill its promises. That's true of all sins, all examples of "My will be done" instead of "Thy will be done." The joys that God wills are true joys. And so the sufferings that God wills, though they are real sufferings, are also true joys and can be known as true joys, not only in the heavenly future but even in the earthly present.

That is why Saint James says, "Count [i.e., reckon, judge, know] it all joy, my brethren, when you meet various trials, for you know that the testing of your faith [by suffering] produces steadfastness ... [so] that you may be perfect and complete [and this includes perfect and complete joy], lacking in nothing" (1:2–4).

Some fake joys, such as drugs, can give us fake mystical experiences, fake ecstasies. You don't really stand outside yourself but exactly the opposite: only further inside yourself. There is no divine Other there.

Christ is our true joy. If we are in Christ and Christ is in us, we can "count it all joy", as James says, even our trials, because they are from God and for God: from God's wise and loving will and for God's glory and even God's joy, as well as ours. For God takes joy in our joy, since "God is love", and that is one of the things that love does: it actively and freely rejoices in the joy of its beloved.

We can even take joy in the fact that we do not feel the joy most of the time when we suffer, for that not-feeling is no accident but is part of God's will for us, His training program for us and our greater joy.

That precious truth, even if firmly believed, may not help our feelings much. But we know much more than we feel. If we don't know any more than we feel, we are not rational animals, just animals. It's our reason (mind, intellect, understanding) that makes us distinctively human. God's revelation to us consists in knowledge, in truth, not in feelings. Much knowledge comes by reason; much more comes by faith.

Even the knowledge of that fact may not influence our feelings, though I think it's bound to, at least gradually and subconsciously. But even if it doesn't, it's still a fact, and we can know it. What we *know* is objectively real, independent of us (we can't *know* what is not real); what we subjectively *feel* is not necessarily real, since appearances are not identical with reality. "There are more things in heaven and earth, Horatio, than are dreamt of in your philosophy."[1]

[1] William Shakespeare, *Hamlet*, ed. Joseph Pearce, Ignatius Critical Editions (San Francisco: Ignatius Press, 2008), act 1, scene 5, lines 166–67.

22

Only Two Philosophies of Joy

The image of being surrounded by a greater reality can apply to many things. For instance, man is surrounded by God, not vice versa. The body is surrounded by the soul, not vice versa, for the soul gives life and meaning to the body. Continents are surrounded by oceans. When we think of oceans, we think of something greater and, therefore, mysterious, uncertain, and insecure, while land naturally symbolizes what is solid, certain, and secure. On this planet, as continents are surrounded by the larger reality of oceans, rather than vice versa, security is surrounded by the greater reality of mystery.

How does this apply to joy and sorrow? Which is surrounded by which?

Pain is relative to pleasure, as disease is relative to health and death to life. We do not say we are restored to disease when we lose our health or restored to death when we lose life. Pleasure and happiness are the norm against which we judge pain and misery.

To live is to be happy. That is why dogs wag their tails and why babies laugh. (What are they laughing at? When they laugh at every thing, they are really laughing at Everything.) Our natural, rightful condition is happiness. The fact that we may be unhappy more often than we are happy means that we are not in our right mind, our natural, God-designed condition. It is an indication of the state theologians call Original Sin. This is true of the lower happiness of pleasure and also of the higher happiness of joy. Sorrow is surrounded by joy, not joy by sorrow. Sorrow is a hole in the ground, not the ground. It is a bump in the road, not the road. It is an interruption.

Look at the parallel here: the continents being surrounded by the sea are a natural image of our little certainties being surrounded by a greater mystery. And since our temporary, particular sorrows are surrounded by and defined by a greater joy, that means that joy, not sorrow, is the great mystery. We understand what sorrow is, but we do not understand what joy is. The greater the sorrow, the clearer is the cause; the greater the joy, the more mysterious is the cause.

Pessimism and nihilism are the opposite philosophy, the normalization of sorrow and the reduction of joy to an accident. This is the philosophy of the Devil, of Arthur Schopenhauer, and of the "Un-man" in C.S. Lewis' novel *Perelandra*: that life and light and love, pleasure and happiness and joy, goodness and truth and beauty are only the thin "rind" surrounding infinite emptiness, like the stretched surface of an inflated balloon, inevitably destined to break and plunge us down into the ultimate truth of nothingness, the triumph of nonbeing over being. The Devil's ultimate philosophy is that of Mephistopheles in Johann Wolfgang von Goethe's *Faust*: "Everything that exists deserves to perish." (That was one of Karl Marx's favorite quotations!)

Joy must have the last word because joy is our response to life, light, and love; to *zoe*, *phos*, and *agape*; to *sat*, *chit*, and *ananda*; to Being, Truth, and Goodness; to Father, Son, and Holy Spirit.

Joy surrounds us like Mary's motherly arms surrounding her Son in typical Christian art—even in the *Pietà*, when

Christ is dead! If we are "in Christ", Mary's motherhood surrounds us too, even if Simeon's sword pierces her soul (Lk 2:35) as Longinus' lance pierces Christ's side (Jn 19:34). We are surrounded by joy even when we feel terror, despair, or agony. We do not feel the joy because it is too big, like the universe, not because it is so small, like a subatomic particle. Joy, not sorrow, is the great mystery. Sorrow can be only finite, but joy can be infinite, for God is joy!

23

How Joy Is Mystical

What is common to joy, mystical experience, sexual intercourse, *agape* love, beauty, and humor?

They all take us out of ourselves. They give us not
just out-of-the-body experiences but out-of-the-mind
experiences. They enable us to stand outside ourselves
(*ek-stasis*). This ecstasy is the meaning, end, purpose, fulfillment, and consummation of our existence. That is why
we were created. And that is how we are made in the
image of God the Trinity, in which each divine Person
exists in and for the others, not just in Himself. Each gives
the ultimate gift, the gift of Himself. That is the nature
of Ultimate Reality, and therefore, it is also the nature of
proximate reality (man, God's image) unless and until it
"falls" away from this metaphysical *agape* into sin, separation, and selfishness. All three s-words are negative, words
of nonbeing, even though selfishness appears to our fallen
consciousness as positive and a way to joy.

Agape is universal, cosmic. Every being gives itself to
other beings in some way. Even a rock takes up space and
blocks other matter, whether as a convenient protection
from arrows or bullets or as an inconvenient obstacle to
one's journey. Jacques Maritain calls this universal self-
giving "ontological generosity". It exists in every being, but
it reaches its height in us, in consciousness and freedom,

in the only being God created in His own image, man, who is the priest of all creation because, by his knowledge and free choice, he can offer the whole known and loved universe to God—or not.

That is why masturbation is bad: it substitutes the self for the other as the object of erotic love. It is bad for the same reason selfish behavior in general is bad. Even if it does not hurt another, it hurts the self in frustrating the self's inherent and essential telos, destiny, and purpose. It gives a fake joy, a false joy, a "mis-leading" joy, a joy that leads in the opposite direction from its natural and God-designed end: inward instead of outward, self-conscious instead of unselfconscious. Imagined others are not real others.

That is also why, when it is good, sex is so very, very good and joyful—total self-giving in both body and soul. That is also why when it is bad, it is so destructive. "Lilies that fester smell far worse than weeds."[1] Sex is a God-designed image of mystical experience; for God created bodies in order to manifest truths about souls, and of all the bodies in the universe, the human body manifests the most. That is why "male and female" is an essential part of "the image of God" (Gen 1:27) and why the confusion, weakening, and destruction of both femininity and masculinity, and of their otherness, is so disastrous today.

It's all in Pope Saint John Paul II's Theology of the Body. Check it out; it's wonderful, and it's the Church's answer to the "sexual revolution". Whenever there is a new lie, the Church teaches the old truth in a new way; whenever there is a destructive heresy, the Church offers a theological correction and deeper explanation; whenever there is a new spiritual pandemic, the Church invents a remedy. Whenever the Devil succeeds in twisting something

---

[1] William Shakespeare, "Sonnet 94", line 14.

beautiful that God created, the Church untwists it so that it emerges stronger, clearer, and more beautiful than ever. That principle applies even to sin and death, which God allows in order to bring about a greater good and a greater life in the end, if only we will it and choose it. That is His surprising, dramatic, and unpredictable answer to "the problem of evil".

24

How Big Is Joy?

How big is joy? Let Saint Anselm tell you. In the last two chapters of his twelfth-century masterpiece, the *Proslogium*, he describes the joy of our union with God in Heaven:

Rouse up, now, my soul, and straighten up your whole understanding ... [of] the one thing necessary in which there is every good.... O the one who enjoys this Good! What will it be to him, and what will it not be? Certainly whatever he wills will be, and that which he wills against will not be. Indeed, goods of the body and the soul will be there, of the sort that neither eye has seen nor ear heard nor the heart of man has thought. Why, therefore, do you wander through many things, little man, in seeking the goods of your soul and body? Love one good, in which all goods are, and it suffices. Desire the simple good, which is every good, and it is enough. For what do you love, what do you desire, my soul? It is there; whatever you love, whatever you desire, is there....

Ask your inmost being if it can grasp the joy it has from so much blessedness belonging to it. But certainly if anyone else whom you love altogether as yourself were to have the same blessedness, your joy would be doubled, because you would rejoice no less for him than for yourself.... Therefore, in that complete charity of the innumerable blessed angels and men, where no one loves

another less than oneself, everyone will rejoice no differently for each other than for oneself. If, therefore, the
heart of man will barely grasp the joy it has from its own
good alone, in what manner will it be capable of so many
and such great joys? . . .

But if they love God with their whole heart, whole
mind, whole soul, yet such that the whole heart, whole
mind, whole soul does not suffice for the dignity of that
love, then surely they will rejoice with their whole heart,
whole mind, whole soul, such that the whole heart, whole
mind, whole soul does not suffice for the fullness of grace.

My God and my Lord, my hope and the joy of my
heart, say to my soul whether this is the joy about which
you spoke to us through your Son: Ask and you will
receive, that your joy may be full. For I have come upon
a certain full joy, and one more than full. Indeed, with
heart full, mind full, soul full, the whole man full of joy,
joy will still exceed above measure. It is not, therefore,
that that whole joy will enter into those rejoicing, but that
all those rejoicing will enter into joy. . . . This is the joy in
which your servants will enter, who enter into the joy of
their Lord.

Human joy is smaller than the whole that we are. It can
enter us, and it can leave us. Divine joy is larger than the
whole that we are. When it enters into us, it is like the air
entering into a flying bird or the ocean into a fish: we are
really entering into it. And unlike human joy, it will never
leave us.

25

What of Agony? How Can That Be Joy?

All this stuff about joy sounds wonderful, but it also seems fragile, for even when joy comes for a while, it also always seems to leave us, to be replaced with emptiness, boredom, sorrow, or even agony. What then?

Sister Wendy Beckett shows us the answer, in *The Mystery of Love*, in meditating on the juxtaposition of a sky-blue crucifix with Christ's most terrible prayer, "My God, my God, why have you forsaken me?" (Mt 27:46). She says,

> Suffering and death are never ... obstacles to fullness of being. They become so, all too often, because we refuse to give up our will and to seek in the pain the divine meaning. Jesus trusted his father too absolutely not to hold in faith that the agony was life-giving.
>
> He experienced, Scripture suggests, unrelieved anguish, including the astonishing sense (almost beyond our imagination) that he had been "forsaken". Yet Jesus clung in faith to the certainty that this was [only] how it *felt*. It could not be how it *was* because the father can never forsake those who love him.
>
> Relying then on nothing human, on no feeling or consolation, exposed to the naked truth of faith, Jesus is set free to soar into total joy.[1]

[1] Sister Wendy Beckett, *The Mystery of Love: Saints in Art through the Centuries* (San Francisco: HarperSanFrancisco, 1996), 70.

Even when we do not attain this sky-blue, soaring freedom—the freedom not from our feelings but from relying on our feelings—we can have this same faith and this same certainty. Note the juxtaposition of the words "faith" and "certainty". This Christian meaning of "faith" is the opposite of the pagan meaning. The Greek word for "faith" is *pistis*, which, for the pagan philosophers, signified a mere opinion that is *not* a certainty.

This distinctively Christian meaning of "faith" is derived from the distinctively Christian *object* of faith—namely, the God who, unlike all the gods of paganism, can neither deceive nor be deceived because He is not made in our image. Little we humans say is absolutely certain; everything God says is. And the words of God are especially certain when spoken by the Word of God personally.

And His last words to us, in Matthew's Gospel, constitute a solemn promise: "Behold, I am with you always, to the close of the age" (28:20). As He said to His disciples in the midst of the terrifying storm at sea, "It is I; have no fear" (14:27). That is the rock-solid foundation for our joy. It is not a principle but a Person.

When life turns sour, the temptation naturally appears to doubt God's existence, His love, His attention, or His power. There seems to be plenty of reasonable evidence to doubt Him. But to abandon our life preserver when our boat is sinking is the most *un*reasonable thing we could possibly do.

26

Joy and Hope versus Entropy

Joy is intimately connected with hope. But this seems to contradict the most fundamental law of the behavior of everything in the universe—namely, entropy, the flow of all energy from higher to lower points of concentration, from order to disorder. It's the second law of thermodynamics. Eventually, the universe will be homogenized. Those who dream of absolute equity will have their Utopia after a few trillion years. What God did in creating the universe, according to Genesis, in *distinguishing* light from darkness, day from night, sky from earth, land from sea, living from nonliving, one species from another, and, within mankind, man from woman will be undone. There will be no "verse" in the "universe", only "uni". One step toward that entropy is to undo the otherness in us ("male and female"), which images the otherness in the Trinity.

Entropy is why hot coffee cools down and cold drinks warm up to room temperature, and why every room in your house gets dirtier and dustier so that, to keep order, you have to keep cleaning it. To keep a white house white, you have to paint it every few years. If you want to be a conservative, you have to keep having revolutions. To keep things the same, you have to keep changing them, repairing them. Our bodies, too, need constant repair, by eating. If we neglect them, we die.

To do nothing is to move inexorably to the disorder that is death. As Samuel Beckett poignantly puts it, "They give birth astride of a grave."[1] All we can do is postpone the inevitable. This truth, blissfully ignored in youth, becomes increasingly obvious as we age.

If we leave things alone, they will decay. If we do nothing, we will gradually become nothing. All progress, and all hope for joy, requires our action. Without our effort, the universe is a failure, not a work of art.

This raises a provocative question: How did evolution, which moves from less order to more, happen in such a universe? There must be a higher force than the physical universe alone to counter entropy. More cannot come from less, so order can't come simply from disorder. True, oak trees grow from acorns, and oak trees are greater than acorns, but those acorns also came from oak trees, which are greater than acorns. An egg is a chicken's way of making more chickens, but a chicken is also an egg's way of making more eggs. Neither chicken nor egg came first; both came from a designing, ordering Mind that stands outside evolution. Computers do not evolve from adding machines; both come from people with minds and wills, not from purely natural forces. In other words, even human reason is relatively supernatural. Nature alone always winds down—even the sun will die—but spirit does not. Only its human bodily container does.

Buddha saw that entropy ruled the universe, and he did not believe we had souls or selves with a supernatural origin, nature, or destiny, so he gave us no hope for the universe or for our bodies or minds, both of which he saw as simply parts of the whole universe, "strands" (*skandhas*)

[1] Samuel Beckett, *Waiting for Godot: A Tragicomedy in Two Acts* (New York: Grove Press, 1954), 103.

woven together like ropes at birth and unwoven at death. His Nirvana is not Heaven: it is not individual, personal, or conscious human life after death. All we can hope for if we are Buddhists is to end suffering by ending its cause: personal desire. (Yet Buddha did call Nirvana "bliss".)

Christianity gives us the "Good News" of the supernatural, the super-entropic, the non-entropic, the more-than-entropic; of bodily resurrection; and of the eternal and infinite progress of the finite human mind, will, and heart into the infinite abyss of divine joy.

27

The Roller Coaster

Every morning I offer God "all my prayers, works, joys, and sufferings of this day". There will be many of all four. Our prayers and works are our gifts to God, and our joys and sufferings are His gifts to us.

Sufferings, too, are gifts because God designed life in this world of matter, time, and space to be a roller coaster of joys and sufferings. It is not Heaven. Here, not only is every down followed by an up, but every up is also eventually followed by a down.

And when it is, we are surprised. And that is the most surprising thing of all: that we question this universal and natural structure of our lives. We do not take suffering and sorrow for granted; we are surprised and outraged by them. We "do not go gentle into that good night". We "rage, rage against the dying of the light".[1] Why? We are not usually surprised by pleasure and happiness. We take them for granted. Why? Why do we expect Heaven on earth instead of the roller coaster? Why do we have a restless heart and a lover's quarrel with the world? (The answer, of course, is because we are not made for this world but for God. This world is only our womb, or our playpen.)

[1] Dylan Thomas, "Do Not Go Gentle into That Good Night", *The Poems of Dylan Thomas*, ed. Daniel Jones (New York: New Directions, 1952), 239.

We ask, If God loves us so much, why didn't He give us constant joy in this world? The answer is that He did, and we fell from that Paradise. Now we cannot appreciate joys without the contrast. In Heaven, our redeemed nature will not need that contrast anymore. But we cannot now imagine that heavenly condition; it is so far from our present experience, inconceivable by "the heart of man" (1 Cor 2:9). We can only believe in it and hope for it. We don't really know what we deeply want, only what we don't want.

If God didn't give us sufferings, we would stagnate. Sufferings are like the bottom of a wave, the trough: that's where the power and energy are. The top of the wave, the crest, is where the ease and delight are.

So the next time God gives you joy, thank Him, but also be wise enough to know that it will not last, that sorrow and suffering are ahead. All roads turn. Tragedy will surprise you tomorrow as joy surprised you today. And if God gives you suffering, know that this, too, will not last and that joy and deliverance will come tomorrow. Every day ends in nightfall, and every night ends in morning. Neither night nor day lasts in this world; what last are two things: the roller coaster and God's loving will, which is the source of both the ups and the downs in this life— which will soon be past! (My grandmother had a hauntingly effective sign on her wall, in needlepoint, that said, "Only one life. 'Twill soon be past. Only what's done for Christ will last.")

The darkness, the nights, the sufferings, the downs, the evils of all kinds do not come from God's "dark side" because He has no dark side. "God is light and in him is no darkness at all" (1 Jn 1:5). They come from the Devil and from our own fallenness. But they are permitted and used by God, who, like a judo master, uses the strength

of his opponent against him. God did this most defini-
tively on Calvary. If He can take the greatest evil that ever
happened, the torture and murder of God Incarnate, and
make of it the greatest good that ever happened, the salvation of the world (our *Good* Friday), He can do the same
with every other comparatively little evil in our lives and
eventually with the roller coaster itself, which, after death,
He will turn into a rocket.

28

Evangelization through Joy

Evangelization is not merely for evangelists. It is not one of many tasks of Christ's Church; it is the primary vocation of all Christians. That sounds like an exaggeration, but here is the proof: What are we here in this world for? To love and help and do good to one another. Our commandment is to "love your neighbor as yourself" (Mt 19:19). So if your primary goal for yourself is to be "born again" with *zoe*—divine life, eternal life—and thus get into Heaven (as the primary goal of a fetus is to be born and thus to get into this world), then that is also your primary goal for your neighbor.

But how can we best achieve that goal? What is the best argument for the evangelist to use when telling the Good News? The most effective one is joy. It's irresistible because it's what everyone deeply wants. We can put up walls of argument against arguments, but we can't argue with joy. The thick walls of our ego, our castle "keep", can stop armies of invaders, but we cannot stop the water that seeps under our castle walls. Joy works like water, not like weapons.

Joy is magnetic. There is an iron filing in every human heart. That's why we find joy "moving" us. The pagan Romans could ignore or scorn Christians' arguments, but they could not ignore or scorn their joy. It was like a miracle. It was, literally, a miracle: it was something supernatural and real, not just another pagan myth but a historical fact, as real as Jesus Himself. In fact, it *was* Jesus Himself in His people, His Mystical Body.

How do we get this joy? Well, it's really very simple. How do you get wet? You go where it's raining. To get the joy of Christ, you go where He is: in His Church; in His sacraments, especially Baptism and the Eucharist; and in prayer, for He is really there too. And He is not deaf or dumb or distant or detached.

The reason the Church's evangelization has been failing in the West (though not in the rest of the world!) is that we don't have Christ's holy joy, and you can't give what you don't have. The Church is growing powerfully in Africa, in China, and even in Muslim countries because it has joy amid its persecutions, poverty, and political pressures. We in the West have far more freedoms and security, yet we have far fewer conversions, fewer saints, fewer martyrs, and fewer miracles. All four of these come not from us but from God; that is why they come not only with supernatural power but also with supernatural joy. Once Christianity becomes as unfashionable and dangerous here as it is in those other places, it will rise again. Once we are close enough to Christ to be passionately hated, we will also be close enough to Christ to be passionately loved. Until then, we will just be half-cooked noodles at room temperature.

29

The Simplest Concrete Icon of Joy

When Jesus wanted to show His disciples a model to imitate in order to enter His Kingdom, He chose a small child (Mt 18:1–4).

Do you want to see, with your physical eyes, something close to simple, complete joy? Then look at the expression on the face of a very small child, who cannot even speak yet, as he looks up into the smiling face of his mother from his position in his mother's cradling arms. What do we see there? Look at that look. We see faith, trust, hope, love, peace, and joy. The baby's face is those things made visible. And not only that, but we see there, as we probably see nowhere else on earth, the *unity*, the oneness, of these things. We see that *they are really all one thing*, as God is one. We see not just faith and trust and hope and love and peace and joy but faith-trust-hope-love-peace-joy. Sometimes we see profound things best when we look at their simplest and most primitive forms.

The source of the joy and peace on the baby's face is the love he is both giving and receiving. The love, in turn, is based on his faith and trust in his mother. That's all. It's simple and pure. Of course, our faith-trust-hope-love-peace-joy has to grow, through struggle, so it cannot be like that of the baby anymore. Or can it? Yes, it not only *can* but also *must* be like that at its center, however much it is covered by complications, as a pearl is covered by an oyster. That pearl is God's own life.

I could use the abstractions and distinctions and principles of philosophy and psychology to try to explain that further, but that would bring us one step further away from the simple unity that we see in that face, both with our eyes and with the eyes of our hearts. For the heart of that baby is not that of some other species; it's your heart too. It's still there and still beating in your breast and smiling under all the covers and complexities of life. That baby is still in us, in all of us, because whatever we once really were, we in some way still are, and can even now hope to be again. I strongly suspect that in Heaven we will have that baby's look toward God, who is our heavenly Father.

And He is our Mother too, for He who invented both fathers and mothers must possess, as their common cause, all the perfections present in both effects. Remember the law of cause and effect: nothing can give what it does not have.

And those two—fatherhood and motherhood, manhood and womanhood—are also perfectly one in Him, since both are His image (Gen 1:27). That image is not described as "male *or* female" (like "Black or White", "old or young", or even "good or evil") but as "male *and* female". "Or" signifies what is accidental; "and" signifies what is essential.

30

Joy Is Ek-static

Ecstasy is not merely a subjective "high". It is an objective, ontological state of being. It means "standing (existing) outside yourself". Not just your feelings or your consciousness but your very being, your identity, your essence, is in some way outside yourself rather than inside. I'm not sure how to explain that logically, but it happens. That's why your identity is often threatened more by another's death than by your own: because you are in the other more than in yourself.

In near-death experiences or out-of-body experiences, people on the brink of life and death often sense themselves outside their bodies, usually floating above them, looking down on them. Their airy bodies sometimes seem to be made of light or some other substance that has no gravity. In mystical experiences, something like that happens to the mind, not (usually) to the body. An authentic mystical experience is a great gift of God, a foretaste of Heaven and of the inner life of God, of the relationship among the three divine Persons, who are totally other-directed and other-centered. The whole being of each, the life and light (thought) and love of each, is in the others. Theologians call this the "circumincession" of the Persons of the Trinity. Their (different) relationships are Their (single) substance.

There are lesser degrees of ecstasy than fully mystical experiences. There is *agape* love, the love that sees the destiny and meaning and importance of your life no longer in yourself but in someone you love. "My life isn't about me. It's about him [or her]." All good parents feel that way about their children. And that is the secret of all good marriages: both husband and wife see themselves that way.

There is also a common experience on the physical level that bears an undeniable, though sometimes embarrassing, similarity to this high and holy thing: sexual intercourse, when orgasm is spiritual as well as physical, when body and soul together leap out of themselves and give themselves to the other.

A much milder form is any pleasant surprise, especially a beautiful personal gift or a suddenly seen natural beauty (a sunset, a sunrise, a thunderstorm, a surf, or a mountain view). It pulls you out of yourself.

Even a fascinating novel or movie can do that. When I was reading *The Lord of the Rings* for the first time, if someone had asked me where I was, I would not have said, "In Boston, in this chair, reading this book" but "In the Shire with the Hobbits fleeing from the Black Riders".

Even the punch line of a joke can surprise us with a delight that takes us out of our former selves, by turning upside down our expectations. Spontaneous laughter is like a tiny mental orgasm.

In fact, all joy is ecstatic, a kind of leap out of our shoes into the air or into the light; and all sorrow is a kind of sinking into oneself, into one's inner darkness and emptiness, like light into a black hole.

All joy is an appetizer of Heaven. And all misery and despair are a warning that there is also a Hell. Joy is God's gift; in fact, it is the gift of Himself, of something of His own life. But a gift is not something automatic or forced. It can be refused. What is freely given must also be freely received. That is the only reason Hell exists.

31

Joy Is the Water, and the Brain
Is a Faucet Handle

The brain works in a surprising way when we have "peak experiences" of joy or of mystical consciousness. (Those two things are not the same, but the brain activity is similar.) Instead of adding some activity, the brain subtracts some. A certain part of the brain stops acting. The brain seems to function, in relation to truth or being or God, as a faucet handle does in relation to water. I think the technical term for that handle is "reducing valve". The faucet is usually acting to stop or to reduce the water that is there from coming in either totally or partially; and the brain is usually acting to *reduce* the consciousness and joy that is there (in God or from God) from overwhelming us and making ordinary rational decisions impossible. That is the brain function that is subtracted, or reduced, in mystical experience. It includes forming words and concepts, and reasoning. All mystics, of all religions (and none), however they differ in explaining and interpreting mystical experience, agree that mystical experience goes beyond reason, words, and concepts.

If there were no faucet handle, no reducing valve, to limit the water the hose brings to us, we would flood or drown. The same is true of spiritual water: truth, being, glory, joy. That is why the joys of this life, like life itself, must be limited. Too much joy would kill us. (But God still gifts us on special occasions with great graces and joys that are much larger than the universe. They are tiny bits of Heaven, still far too big for us to understand or control.)

Here is the theological explanation for the above-mentioned brain functioning. Everything in the universe, everything God created, has in common one point, purpose, telos, task, and end: to express in a finite and material way God's infinite and immaterial perfections, His being, knowing, and willing; His life, light, and love; His beauty, truth, and goodness. God made creatures to share His goodness with them because that's what goodness does: it shares itself, gives itself, diffuses itself, like sunlight, like all energy. He who contained perfect otherness within His own Trinitarian nature and thus needed no others, out of sheer generosity created others, outside Himself. To pour out His infinitude on others, He created others—i.e., finite creatures.

Things are limited by what they are not. Thus, numbers, spaces, times, and bodies exclude and limit one another. All good except God is limited: one finite good is not another good, though all goods are one in God (e.g., His mercy *is* His justice). Physical goods, psychological goods, and even spiritual goods in us are limited by their opposites—by physical, psychological, and spiritual evils: pleasure by pain, happiness by unhappiness, joy by sorrow, life by death, knowledge by ignorance.

God "finitizes" His gifts so that we can receive them. For "whatever is received, is received in the mode of the receiver."[1] A bucket of seawater is the size and shape of the bucket, not of the sea. Thus, the ordinary operation

[1] *ST* I, q. 75, art. 5.

of our brain's "reducing valve" is like God's act of creating: it reduces what is of itself infinite to finite quantities so we can take it in. That is why our joy, though from an infinite source, is, in us, finite. Yet even the tiny bits of it that enter into us in this life can be so intoxicating that they break our hearts. In our joy, we weep because we *leak*: we cannot contain or control what is greater than ourselves. We weep for sorrow too when it is greater than ourselves, e.g., the death of someone we love. Water means both life (Jn 4:14) and death (Noah's flood).

32

Taking Stock: What We Know and What We Don't

We know that God exists. But we do not know His essence. We don't know what He is, only what He isn't. We also know what He is like, or rather what is like Him in a finite way: whatever is true, good, or beautiful. Joy is one of those things.

Let's look at what we know about His three most important attributes: His omnibenevolence, His omniscience, and His omnipotence—His infinite goodness, wisdom, and power, the three attributes that make Romans 8:28 true.

We know that God is omnibenevolent love, not hate or indifference. But we cannot comprehend, even though we can apprehend and believe, these three things: (1) how *much* He loves us (how much is infinity?), (2) *why* He loves us (isn't love its own reason?), and (3) that His gifts of love that don't give us feelings of joy really are gifts of love and for our greater joy in the end (we don't know *how* it works, but we do know *that* it does).

We know that God is omniscient, not ignorant. But we do not know what omniscience is because we don't experience it. It includes knowing everything completely and at once, not step by step or in time. We know ourselves and our universe only a little bit, for we know that we did not design ourselves or create ourselves (though fools keep trying) or our universe.

We know that God is omnipotent. And we know that (but not how) He uses His power most effectively when He seems to withdraw it. We don't understand why He does not perform the miracles that He could perform and that we would perform if we were God—because we're not God. (Call out the reporters! Stop the presses!)

We don't have His wisdom because we are not God. And I think the reason we don't have His wisdom is that we don't have His love. For wisdom depends on love at least as much as love depends on wisdom.

We therefore know that God allows evils in our lives only for the sake of greater goods or to avoid even greater evils (e.g., often He does not give us the grace to overcome lesser sins because that would lead us to the greater sin of pride). But we do not know which evils God will allow in our lives. We only know that He has good reasons for allowing them and that all these reasons come from His wisdom and love. And this is the faith knowledge that is the basis of our joy.

33

Taking Stock: More of What We Know and What We Don't

We know that we want joy, not sorrow. But we know that we will never, in this world, get exactly what we want. How awful that would be!

We know that God is joy and the source of all joy.

We know that we deeply long for some kind of transcendent, total joy in Heaven that we cannot imagine on earth, and we know that God wants to give us that. But we don't know with infallible certainty that we will go to Heaven because that depends on our free choice of faith and hope and charity. But our own faith is not the reliable object of our faith; only God is.

We know that if we choose God and His holy joy, we will get it, for that is His promise, and He never reneges on His promises. But we do not know that we will choose it always or how and when we will get it.

We know that we will have some joys and some sorrows on earth. But we do not know which ones or how large both will be. Our roller coasters are not all the same size, only the same shape.

We know that we will be burdened with some sins (and their miseries) and graced with some virtues (and their joys) on earth. But we do not know how many or which ones.

We don't know our future regresses and progresses on earth. We know that we will be perfected and cleansed by our sufferings, both here (where only some of those sufferings are accepted and made profitable) and in Purgatory (where they all are). But we don't know the extent of those sufferings.

We don't know whether we will need Purgatory before Heaven, but the odds are pretty good. Does New York City need garbage collections?

We know that we will die. But we don't know when or how or what the state of our souls will be at that time.

We know that we will be judged by the God who is unlimited mercy and also total truth and perfect justice. Psalm 85 tells us that mercy and justice ("righteousness", "faithfulness") are reconciled (v. 10) because earth and Heaven are reconciled (v. 11). We now know how: by Christ's Incarnation. Mercy as well as justice will come from God because justice will come from earth as well as from Heaven; from man (Christ as man) as well as from God (Christ as God).

We do not know what words we will hear from God's lips at the Last Judgment. Our hope is that they will be the words of Matthew 25:23. (I'm not going to quote them; read them yourself. I hope you keep a Bible handy when reading this book; it's like keeping the measuring tape handy when you do your carpentry.)

In all these things, which is more important: what we know or what we do not know? If we subtracted all the things we know, how big a subtraction would that be? If we added all the things we do not know, how big an addition would that make? Would it be better if we swapped the two categories, if we knew all the things we don't know now and didn't know all the things we do know? God knows what we need to know.

34

The Trinitarian Basis for Joy

The three greatest joys are life, light, and love: (1) the joy of *being*, receiving the gift of existence and life, (2) the joy of *seeing*, receiving the gift of truth and light, and (3) the joy of *loving*, receiving and giving the gift of love.

The sun symbolizes these three things and their unity. It exists, it gives light, and it gives heat.

The Father is the source of all being, all existence—timelessly, of the coequal Son and Spirit, and temporally, of all creation.

The Son is the self-knowledge of God, the Logos, the Mind of God, the Truth of God, the Word of God, the Light of the world.

The Spirit is the love of God, the love between the Father and the Son.

These three, though three Persons and thus distinct, are also absolutely one: one being, one substance, one essence, one divine nature, one God. God is so one that in Him everything is one; every attribute is one with every other attribute. In Him, being and knowing and loving are one: to be *is* to know *is* to love. They are not in a causal relationship. God is all cause, not effect. The whole God is the whole cause of all effects, all created things.

In us (even the saints), being, knowing, and loving are not wholly one. They are three colors of the spectrum made by the single light, the light that transcends colors, being refracted into three different colors by the prism of creation.

Thus, our joy is also threefold: life, light, and love in English; *zoe*, *phos*, and *agape* in Greek; *sat*, *chit*, and *ananda* in Sanskrit. Simply to be, to be alive, is a joy. Simply to know, to see, to understand, to contemplate, is a joy. And simply to be "in" love is a joy. Three different joys.

In Heaven, they will also be one single joy.

Without losing our finitude, our humanity, and without losing the distinction between these three things, light and life and love, we will also share in a finite way in God's oneness of these three things. For we will participate in the divine nature (2 Pet 1:4). Christ became like us so that we could become like Him.

35

Joy's Trinity

Joy is one of the fruits of the Holy Spirit. It is the second one listed, in fact, after love (charity, *agape*) (Gal 5:22–23).

The Holy Spirit is the Spirit *of the Father and of the Son.*

And Christ is the Son *of the Father.* He says, "He who has seen me has seen the Father" (Jn 14:9).

Thus, he who has known the Holy Spirit has also known the Son and the Father.

The Spirit does not add to Christ or subtract anything from Christ; He reveals Christ, just as Christ does not add to or subtract from the Father but reveals the Father. "In him all the fulness of God was pleased to dwell" (Col 1:19).

The three Persons are not "parts" of God. God has no parts.

We receive all God's gifts, including joy, from all three Persons, as we receive love and peace and salvation from Them. There is no "specialization" in God Himself but only in relation to us.

Creation is most directly and especially, but not exclusively, the work of God the Father. But the Father created by means of His Word, and it was His Spirit who formed and shaped creation (Gen 1:1–3).

Justification is most directly and especially, but not exclusively, the work of the Son, on the cross. The Father and the Spirit act here too, for it was the Father's will that

Christ was incarnated and died, and He was led by the Spirit to do all that He did.

Sanctification is most directly and especially, but not exclusively, the work of the Spirit, for the Spirit "internalizes" the work of the Father and the Son in our lives. He makes the Father's love more intimate in our souls, as the Son made the Father's love more intimate in our world, our community, His Church. The Holy Spirit is the soul of the Church.

Love seeks maximum intimacy, maximum union. The three stages of salvation history in time are stages of increasing intimacy (the Father above us, the Son beside us, the Spirit within us), not because God increases but because we do.

The Father was creation's efficient cause, or origin; the Son was creation's formal cause, or design; and the Spirit was creation's final cause, or perfection. Our joy, therefore, has three reasons in God: (1) that God the Father is our Father too, (2) that God the Son is our Savior and our brother, and (3) that their Spirit, God's loving heart, lives at the heart of our hearts. The Spirit shares with us God's heart (and therefore God's love and therefore God's joy), as the Son shares with us God's mind (Phil 2:5).

This is not imitation but incorporation. Imitation is "monkey business", like apes trying to play musical instruments designed for humans. Imitation may be a search for joy, but incorporation *is* joy.

36

Joy's Place and Order among the Fruits of the Spirit

The fruits of the Spirit are listed in a deliberate order, beginning with "love, joy, peace" (Gal 5:22–23). Joy's place is second. Peace depends on joy, and joy depends on love. Peace depends on joy because sorrow is, by its essential nature, warlike, rebellious, not at peace with itself. And joy depends on love because all who are loveless are also joyless.

Joy is number two in importance, then. It is also number two in causal order. Love causes joy. Joy, in turn, causes peace. No need for war when we are in loving union with God, self, and neighbor rather than with the Devil, the flesh, and the world—that is, with pride, lust, and greed, whose enemies are obedience, chastity, and poverty. The list is not arbitrary; there is a structural order here. Our three enemies are the world, the flesh, and the Devil; peace with the world is greed, peace with the flesh is lust, and peace with the Devil is pride. The three vows of poverty, chastity, and obedience are the enemies of greed, lust, and pride, respectively. They are the enemies of our enemies. Peace with God overcomes the Devil and pride; peace with ourselves overcomes the flesh and lust; peace with our neighbors overcomes the world (fallen human society) and greed.

Our relations with others, self, and God are also hierarchically ordered. Thomas Merton writes, "We cannot be at peace with others because we are not at peace with ourselves, and we cannot be at peace with ourselves because we are not at peace with God."[1] That is the fundamental principle of Christian psychology.

Don't reverse the order. Don't put peace first or love last. Love is first because love brings us out of ourselves the most, and this ek-stasis (standing outside ourselves) gives us the most ecstasy (joy). We are most in joy when we en-joy the other, not the self; when we are the most unselfconscious.

Peace comes third—at the end, not at the beginning. We do not begin in peace; we "rest in peace". Augustine pointed out that peace is essentially positive, the fulfillment of our inherent purpose, the rest for our restless hearts— not negative, the absence of war. We are at peace when we have joy, which is what we most deeply seek; and we have joy when we live in love, which is what we most deeply need. Wisdom is the conforming of our wants to our needs.

---

[1] Thomas Merton, *The Living Bread* (New York: Farrar, Straus & Giroux, 1956), xiii.

37

Does God Enjoy Our Joys?

What is God's attitude toward our thousands of little "secular" joys, such as delicious food and human companionship and bright, sunny days and beautiful landscapes and the feel of waves of cold salt water at the beach and a hot bath on a cold winter day? Is He too high and holy and heavenly to be involved with us little animals when we are grunting with pleasure?

Whenever we ask a question about God, our very first instinct should be to turn to our most adequate data, to Christ, who reveals the whole of God (Jn 14:9; Col 2:9). Christ participated in ordinary human pleasures, such as weddings and banquets (Jn 2:1–12; 12:2; Lk 7:31–50), and was criticized for this by the joyless Pharisees (Lk 7:34).

According to His own inspired Scriptures, God "rejoices" in us as well as in Himself (Is 62:5). There are at least three reasons why God approves and enjoys our human joys. First, He designed them for us. He designed the whole world for us, the whole unimaginably enormous universe, in fact. We can't live in the rest of it, only on this planet, but the whole universe is a sign; it is significant; it is designed for us, in that it reveals to us the two great truths of God's immensity and our tininess. Everything that exists is planned, part of a work of art. For God is not *a* god. Nothing happens, not the fall of a sparrow, a hair, or a subatomic particle, without His will. Thus, He designed our sufferings, too, for our greater joy; for God is love, and love's aim is the joy of the beloved. Even in a story crafted by a competent merely human author, there are no accidents. Even the randomness in the story is *designed* by the author. Not a syllable is inserted by his cat, his pen, or his mother. How could the divine Author of the whole story lack what human authors have?

As Thornton Wilder says, at the end of part 1 of *The Bridge of San Luis Rey*, there are only two possible philosophies of everything: "Some say that ... to the gods we are like the flies that the boys kill on a summer day, and some say, on the contrary, that the very sparrows do not lose a feather that has not been brushed away by the finger of God."[1]

A second reason God knows and feels our joys is that He has a heart as well as a mind. He even has feelings. Not all feelings are essentially material or temporal or passive "passions", and joy (insofar as joy is a feeling) is one of them. So is love. Both joy and love are more than feelings, but they are (active) feelings too.

God does not change, like romantic lovers, or wear away, like the statues of sculptors. God is love, complete love itself; that is why He does not fall in love: for the same reason water does not get wet. God is active, but He does not change, because not all activity is change. Some activities continue unchanging; for instance, Christ unchangeably "hides" (*latens*) behind the appearances of bread and wine in the Eucharist; it is an unchanging activity. Hiding is an activity; it is what He is *doing* there. God is always active.

[1] Thornton Wilder, *The Bridge of San Luis Rey* (New York: Grosset & Dunlap, 1927), 23.

A third reason God enjoys our joys is that the Ascension was not the undoing of the Incarnation. Therefore, the human nature of Christ, with its human emotions *and even its passive emotions*, which are part of human nature, is forever substantially united to His divine nature in that single divine Person, and thus Christ feels all the good passive emotions that we feel. He also actively empathizes with all our sorrows.

So the next time you notice yourself smiling at some earthly joy, remember that Christ is smiling and en-joying too. Is He with us any *less* than our human friends are? Our enjoying His gifts is part of His human joy.

38

Three Levels of Reality and Joy

All religions, all cultures, and all men know innately and instinctively that there are three levels of reality: ourselves, what is greater than ourselves, and what is less than ourselves. In other words, man, God, and nature, or the universe.

All who are wise also know that the heart, the power to love, is the deepest thing in ourselves. "From [the heart] flow the springs of life", says Solomon (Prov 4:23). That is why the very first question Jesus asks us in John's Gospel is "What do you seek?" (Jn 1:38). In other words, what do you love?

Put these two points together and you get the conclusion that the three things we can seek and love are thus (1) the supernatural good that transcends us, (2) the personal good that is in us (and in our neighbors), and (3) the cosmic good that surrounds us.

The good above us is God Himself. Since He is the greatest good, He is also the greatest joy. His joy is not a static perfection but a dynamic, active, willful more-than-perfection, a more-than-fullness. It is the ecstasy of *agape*.

Our personal good is an image of that because we are made "in God's image". Mirroring God's ek-static overflow, it is our overflow, our self-transcendence, our God-like joy. Our learning and attaining that joy is what God allows all our sufferings *for*. His love-joy is in love with us and therefore with our love-joy.

That is why all our prayers, works, joys, and sufferings of every day should be offered up to Him and His will. To will His will is to will our own supreme joy *because that is what He wills*: our supreme joy.

The cosmic good is the *glory* of God in all things, God "all in all" (Eph 1:23). Streaming throughout the world and filling all things is His sunlight, which mirrors His Sonlight. This includes the floods and the trees, both of which "clap their hands" in aquatic and arboreal joy (Ps 98:8; Is 55:12).

Thus, the pagan, pantheistic, and Romanticist longing for the self-transcending joy of becoming mystically one with nature is fulfilled only by our total surrender to the transcendent Creator of nature and of ourselves. The only way to get into the heart of the art is to get into the heart of the Artist.

Two joys that are even greater—incomparably greater—than this joy of entering into the heart of God's creation are entering into the heart of another human heart and entering into the heart of God, as revealed most completely in Christ.

39

Why Isn't the Way to Joy Simple
and Easy to Find?

Despite what we may think, the way to joy *is* easy to find! It's scandalously simple, and it is universal (true everywhere) and unchangeable (true everywhen) and total (lacking nothing) and perfect (unsurpassable) and concrete (not abstract) and practical (it really works). It is *faith*: to believe everything the infallible God tells us, with no nuances, no little scholarly dances, no mitigations and qualifications and relativizations and reductionisms and subjectivizations. It is the knowledge, by faith (faith is a kind of knowledge), of the fact that every thing and every event in the universe speaks to us the same simple message, the same word from the Word of God, the Mind of God, the Logos, the Light of God, the Sun of God, the Son of God, the Light of the world: "It is I; do not be afraid" (Jn 6:20). He is *with* us in everything.

This knowledge comes by faith, not by proof. But it is the most certain knowledge we can have because it comes from God; it is revealed by God, who is the only One who can never deceive or be deceived.

"It is I; do not be afraid"—Christ spoke those words to His disciples in the middle of the night, the darkness, the storm, and the terror. All the more clearly does He speak those words to us in the sunlight. Let us simply stay with that short and simple fact, the fact of Him, of His presence, of His mastery of all things. "All authority in heaven and on earth has been given to me", He says in Matthew 28:18. Let's stay with that fact instead of trying to add to it (which is impossible) or qualify it (why would one want to do that?) or explain it (by what higher principle could it be explained?) or argue for it and deduce it (but from what? It is Alpha and Omega; *He* is Alpha and Omega [Rev 22:13]). Let us stay with it, for it stays with us. It's not an "it"; it's a "He". Let us stay there, with Him. He is all we need, and therefore He can be and should be all we want. Say to Him what the most brilliant and sophisticated philosopher and theologian who ever lived said to Him. When He said to Saint Thomas Aquinas, "You have written well of me, Thomas. What will you have as your reward?", Saint Thomas' answer was the best and simplest possible: *Non nisi te, Domine.* "Only Thyself, Lord."

The way to joy is so terribly simple and wonderful that the Devil has to make it complicated or abstract or boring or uncertain or mythological or scholarly to turn our eyes away from its light. He can't simply deny it and tell us that God is evil and the Devil is good—that is so clearly a lie that it would provoke us to faith. So he has to cover it up, muffle it, shuffle it, and ruffle it. His most effective technique is not to say no to it but to say "yes but". He puts a "but" after it—a big butt, his butt. And we know what his butt is full of.

40

Why Does the Eucharist Give Us Joy?

The answer to the question of why the Eucharist gives us joy is very simple. The *Catechism of the Catholic Church* says that the Eucharist is both the "source" and the "summit", both the foundation and the fulfillment, of our life in Christ (1324). Why? Because it *is* Christ, in person, really present, the whole of Him, divinity and humanity, and, within His humanity, both soul and body, and, within His body, both the resurrected flesh and the shed blood. The Eucharist gives us joy because the Eucharist is Christ Himself, and Christ Himself is the source of all human joy.

If Christ were to appear here in person, right now, in front of you, and smile at you and call you His beloved son or daughter, what would your reaction be? That should be your reaction to the Eucharist too. It is the closest anyone can ever come in this world to Heaven.

In the Eucharist, there is no "outsideness", only "insideness", of both body and soul. We are no longer outside Him but in Him, and He in us. It is complete "withness", far more perfect and complete than the most perfect experience available in this life, even if, in it, He often hides from our feelings as much as He hides from our eyes.

Adoring Christ in the Eucharist brings joy and power and revival not only to every individual but also to every parish that practices adoration in faith. (And why would anyone ever practice adoration if he did *not* have faith?) If a culture or a nation or a world practiced adoration, it would bring to them also the deepest joy. And God knows, our culture, our nation, and our world could use an injection of joy!

And you don't have to be a public mover and shaker to move and shake our culture. For a culture (or a nation or a world) is literally nothing without the individual persons who make it up, who constitute it. The Church calls herself "the *People* of God". If there are no people, there is no Church. There is no social justice (the supposedly "liberal" or "progressive" thing) without personal justice, charity, and sanctity (the supposedly "conservative" or "traditional" thing). Only the faith of the saints can move mountains. The exact same force that moves mountains in individual lives can move mountains in society. And that force is not what we merely *see* or *know* or *use* but what we *eat* and *become* when we receive the Eucharist. For "you are what you eat."

So stop moaning about our social decay and receive the Answer to it, and then share Him and His joy with all whom you meet. For "the joy of the LORD is your strength" (Neh 8:10).

Nothing tears apart a society more obviously than war. And nothing is more contrary to joy than war. Abortion is the worst form of war. It is the war that comes closest to home. It is not foreign war but civil war—war within the family, war within the womb, war against our own sons and daughters, whom we poison or rip apart. Abortion is the primary issue of social justice in our culture. Abortion is totally empty of joy. The Eucharist is totally full of joy. The Eucharist is the answer to abortion. No one who adores Christ in the Eucharist can commit abortion. No one who believes the words "This is my body" (Mt 26:26; Mk 14:22; Lk 22:19; 1 Cor 11:24) can say those most holy words in her own name to justify the unholy deed of killing her own little child of Jesus in her womb.

41

What Happens in the Eucharist to Give Joy?

It's very simple. In the Eucharist, what looks, tastes, feels, smells, and sounds like bread is not bread. It is Christ Himself, really present, the whole Christ, body and soul, humanity and divinity. Where His body is, His body brings His soul along with it, for His body is never without His soul. A body without a soul is a corpse! And where His soul is, His soul brings His body along with it too, for the same reason: a soul without a body is a ghost. He is risen; He is not dead. His body is not a corpse, and His soul is not a ghost.

He is present in both His divinity and His humanity and, within His humanity, in both soul and body and, within His body, in both flesh and blood. He is just as truly and objectively present here and now as He was on the hellish cross and in the angry streets of Jerusalem and in the protection of His mother's womb.

We receive His divinity with His humanity because His divinity is one with His humanity. We receive His soul with His body because His soul is one with His body. We receive the "bread" and "wine" separately because His flesh and blood were separated in His death. So we receive His death as well as His life.

What is He doing there? He is feeding us, and He is also hiding, in the transubstantiated Host. Hiding is an action.

He is acting to suppress the appearances of His human body and to keep in existence the appearances of the bread and wine, even though the substance or essential nature of the bread and wine is gone, transubstantiated into His Body and Blood. If you saw Him without His disguise, what would you do? After you answer that question, do it now.

You know He knows all things, so you know He knows you. He sees you seeing what appears to be bread and knowing it is He. His gaze is fully on you, even though yours is not fully on Him. Knowing this, what do you say to Him? What would you say to Him if you saw Him face-to-face, if a time machine brought you back two thousand years to His time and place? Well, say it. Because an equally great miracle has happened: a time machine that He invented at the Last Supper, the Eucharist, has brought Him forward to your time and place. The Eucharist is the extension of the Incarnation.

This is not an "as if" but an "is". It is not an analogy or a symbol. He and you are really meeting here and now in three equally true but increasingly intimate ways: in your present act of faith, in eucharistic adoration, and in Holy Communion. So what do you say to Him? Stop reading this page and answer that question. Speak your words to Him. Take your time. Don't read another line until you have done that single most important thing you could possibly do while reading this book.

Are you back? OK. Now, after looking at Him, look at your joy. And you can do that every single day, if you live near a Catholic church! You can eat Him; you can eat divine joy; you can eat the meaning of life.

Scripture's description of Heaven—"No eye has seen, nor ear heard, nor the heart of man conceived, what God has prepared for those who love him" (1 Cor 2:9)—applies as literally to the Eucharist as to Heaven.

42

That's Great, but What If I Don't Feel the Joy?

You know, that is a really stupid question! (I am as harsh with myself as I am with you, dear reader, for that really stupid question sometimes arises in my mind also.) Why is it stupid? Because what we lack—the feeling—compared with what we have—God in the flesh—is like a flea compared with a galaxy. And what we have cannot at all depend on what we lack; His real presence cannot possibly depend at all on our feelings. He is not a dream or an illusion or a therapy or a thought experiment or a fiction or an invention or a creative imagination; He is God! He brought Himself and us together for this meeting not to change our feelings but to change our being.

How much has He desired this meeting? He told us, on Holy Thursday when He instituted this sacrament. He said, "I have earnestly desired to eat this Passover with you before I suffer" (Lk 22:15).

And how far has He brought you so that you can meet Him thus? From absolute nothingness, by creating the universe and using it to make the unique and irreplaceable person that is you, by an incredibly complex providential plot, through all the 13.7 billion years of the history of the cosmos, and through all the apparently random changes in biological evolution, and through all the apparent accidents of history, and through all the marriages of all your ancestors, and through the unlikely selection of one out of twenty million sperm to unite with your mother's ovum, and through all the events of your life, just so that He and you could meet. That's why He created the universe! He brought you from nonexistence, from utter nothingness, to this meeting.

And how far has He has brought Himself for this meeting? From divinity to humanity, from Heaven to earth, from eternal joy to the cross and the tomb.

And in light of all that, you are complaining about your precious little feelings?

Forget yourself and your feelings. They hold less of His joy than a single molecule of salt water holds of the ocean. Forget everything else: it is He, the meaning of all things, the consummation of all things, the Lord of all things, the joy of all things, who now wants all your attention and all your love, as you have all His attention and all His love. All of it—total, infinite, unqualified, eternal, indivisible, unbreakable.

Can we get a sense of proportion here? God must have not only infinite patience with us but also a sense of humor so enormous that if we heard Him laughing, we could not endure it and would just dissolve or collapse or melt away. It's so ridiculous that it's hilariously funny that we have this bug's-eye perspective in the face of the fact that our Creator cracked open the dome of the universe to come down into it, into Mary's womb, into a Crucifixion, into what looks like a little piece of bread, and into our mouths and stomachs, passionately hoping that we would open our hearts as simply and completely as we open our mouths. Fulfill His desire, His thirst. (Google Saint Teresa of Calcutta's meditation on His "I thirst" from the cross. It helped make her a saint, and it will help you too.)

43

Christ Is All "Four Causes" of Our Joy

Christ is the cause of our joy. What does that mean? What does "cause" mean?

Aristotle's idea about the "four causes" is one of the most useful, commonsensical, reasonable ideas that ever occurred to any human mind. It uses the word "cause" in a broader sense than modern English does. It classifies the four possible explanations of all things, the four reasons for anything that is an effect, anything except God:

The formal cause is the true formula of the thing, the essence or essential nature of the thing (or event), the answer to the question "*What* is it?"

The material cause is what the thing is made of, or made from—the potentiality that was actualized when the thing came into existence, when it became actual.

The efficient cause is its maker, source, or origin—its "pusher" into being, to use a physical metaphor.

The final cause is its "puller", its end, good, purpose, point, perfection, fulfillment, flourishing, fruit, value, consummation, goal, aim, telos, or direction. When we ask, "What is the meaning of life?", we are usually asking for its final cause, its value and purpose, its end, its good. (One of the most humanly destructive ideas in the history of philosophy is the typically modern idea that final causes are only subjective, only a projection of our desires, not objectively real.)

So the formal cause is what the thing is made into, the material cause is what the thing is made out of, the efficient cause is what the thing is made by, and the final cause is what the thing is made for.

Christ is the formal cause of our joy because He is what true joy looks like: its essence, definition, archetype, template, touchstone, Platonic Form, ideal, perfection, or standard.

Christ is the material cause of our joy because we are in His material Body, both in the Church and in the Eucharist. Christ is the content of our joy. He is what our joy is "made of".

Christ is the efficient cause of our joy because joy is His grace, His gift. Of course, the Father and the Holy Spirit also share in this work. The three divine Persons never act alone, even when the Son alone becomes incarnate.

Christ is the final cause of our joy because He and His joy are our end, aim, and perfection. We set our sights on Him. He is what we most deeply long for. He defines the direction in which we move and grow. Our joy gradually grows into His, as our love grows into His, and our very life (our *bios*, or natural life) grows into His *zoe*, His supernatural life.

44

The Mystery of Withness

Whenever someone we love is dying, we naturally ask what we can do for him. The best answer, and usually the only answer, is simply to *be* there with him. That is the gift of self, of real presence, personal presence. Only a person can be present. Furniture is not present; it is just there. It does not "present itself" to us. It does not answer the roll call by saying, "Here!" It does not have a proper name unless we personify it—i.e., pretend that it does.

How did God reveal His love to us? By being *with* us, present to us. The Incarnation fulfilled God's prophetic name in Isaiah, the name "Immanu-el", which means "God with us". That is what love seeks: withness, intimacy, closeness, union. Not pleasure, or even happiness, or peace, or contentment, but withness. A true lover says, "Better to be with her [or him] than happy without her [or him]." Many marriages were saved by that choice.

Just as the cause of Heaven's joy is withness, the cause of Hell's misery is aloneness. Plotinus' description of the Heaven of mystical experience was "alone into the Alone" (*Enneads* 6, 6). He couldn't have been more wrong. Sartre wrote, in *No Exit*, the other half of that ultimate lie, that "Hell is other people."

It is not a dogma, but it is a reasonable and probable opinion (a "theologoumenon") that Christ would have become man and entered our world even if we had not fallen and sinned, simply to get closer to us, to fulfill love's longing for union.

In stark contrast to the unity of pantheism or monism, the unity that love seeks includes otherness, being-with-another. That is why God is a Trinity: because He is love, and love (and therefore its joy) requires both oneness and otherness, which is *withness*. Although God is "God alone" in the sense that He is *unique* (there is only one God), He is not alone: He is *with* Himself in the love among the three Persons.

God did not create man because He was lonely. God is not lonely. He is a Trinity, a society, a family. He is absolute perfection, but absolute perfection is not simply oneness but also otherness, manyness, and withness, because ultimate perfection is not just oneness but love. Love is not just a good thing to do and the fundamental value; it is the nature of ultimate reality. It is not only the ethical ultimate; it is also the metaphysical ultimate.

Thus, our supreme joy is His promise: "Behold, I am with you always" (Mt 28:20). "It is I" (Jn 6:20). Meditate on that exceedingly simple truth. Do you really believe it? If your answer is "yes, but ...", then pray, "I believe; help my unbelief!" (Mk 9:24). He will honor that prayer because of the honesty in the first part and because of the love and longing in the second part.

45

What Does the Bible Say about Joy?

How can you find out what Scripture says about joy? Read it! Especially Nehemiah 8:10; Esther 9:22; Job 20:5; 29:13; 38:7; Psalms 5:11; 16:11; 27:6; 30:5; 32:11; 43:4; 48:2; 51:8, 12; 105:43; 126:5; 137:6; Proverbs 12:20; 15:21; 17:21; 21:15; Ecclesiastes 2:26; Isaiah 12:3; 29:19; 35:10; 51:11; Jeremiah 15:16; 31:13; Habakkuk 3:18; Matthew 25:21, 23; 28:8; Luke 1:44; 15:7, 10; 24:41; John 3:29; 15:11; 16:20–22, 24; 17:13; Romans 14:17; 15:13, 32; 2 Corinthians 2:3; Galatians 5:22; Philippians 1:4; 1 Thessalonians 1:6; 2:19–20; Philemon 7; Hebrews 12:2; James 1:2; 4:9; 1 Peter 1:8; 4:13; 1 John 1:4; 2 John 12; 3 John 4; and Jude 24.

That's what God's Book wants us to know about joy. My book is based on His.

46

How Do We Offer Our "Prayers, Works, Joys, and Sufferings"?

In the Morning Offering, I offer to God "all my prayers, works, joys, and sufferings of this day"—not just in general, as an *abstraction*, but "of this day", concretely, where and when I actually live.

It is easy to understand why we offer Him all our *prayers*. The four purposes of prayer are adoration, thanksgiving, repentance and reparation for sin, and petition for our goods, our needs, and those of our neighbors. To whom but God can we direct those intentions?

It is easy to understand why we offer Him all our *works*. Works should be motivated not merely by our good natural and personal motivations but, above all, by the desire to do His will, which largely consists of our ordinary daily duties. That is how we help His Kingdom to come and His will to be done on earth more and more as it is in Heaven.

And it is also fairly easy to understand how our *sufferings* can be offered to God by our acceptance of them as His wise and loving will for us (though this is far more difficult to do than to understand). We do this by our faith in and hope in and love of God and of His perfect providence, thus turning our passive sufferings into active works of faith.

But how are we to offer up our *joys*?

One answer is simple: since sufferings are the opposite of joys, we offer our joys by accepting their absence as God's holy will for us.

A second answer is part of the virtue of hope. We offer our joys to God somewhat as we offer our money to the bank, as a kind of trust and investment in the future, in the greater joys of Heaven.

A third answer is a form of fasting from some of our earthly joys (food is only one of them), thus carving out a hollow place in our hearts that God alone can fill. We need to be "detached" from our dependence on earthly goods and joys in order to be totally "attached" to God. The problem is not those goods themselves, if they are innocent and not sinful, but our addiction to them.

A fourth answer is part of gratitude and thanksgiving. We offer up our joys, as we would offer up a great Christmas present, for our Benefactor to see, and for Him to see our joy in receiving His gift. God enjoys our joys! Our smiles say to God, "See, Daddy, how happy You make me!" This is an expression of gratitude, which is such a fundamental spiritual attitude that without it, there can be no religion at all. Even Buddhism, which knows no God, requires a kind of total, cosmic gratitude, although there is no One for Buddhists to be grateful to. Their hearts are wiser than their theology.

47

The Basis for Our Joy Is
the Nature of God

Omniscience, omnipotence, and omnibenevolence—infinite wisdom, power, and goodness—are the three most important divine attributes, both in theory and in practice: in theory because any being deserving of the name "God" cannot be stupid, weak, or wicked; in practice because only if God possesses all three attributes is Romans 8:28 necessarily true. That most amazing piece of good news logically follows from these three divine attributes, but only if all three are true.

Work that out for yourself. You can see that God's ignorance, weakness, or lovelessness toward us are three easy answers to account for all the evils we experience, both physical and spiritual. There are four easy explanations for evil: no God, dumb God, weak God, or bad God. If we deny all four of these alternatives, we have a fifth answer that is more joyful, hopeful, rich, and mysterious. It is that God's unlimited power, wisdom, and love, taken together, transform all our evils from "downs" into ultimate "ups"—that is, into things that God providentially "works for good" for us.

Even our sins can be used for our greater good if we walk with them through the golden door of repentance. This is why God does not give us the grace immediately to avoid them; they are a medicine against our pride, which would swell and corrupt us if God removed all our other sins. We would then not know from experience our moral weakness, we would not be humble, and we would not have to trust in God's grace and mercy rather than in our own virtue. We would become Pharisees. We would go to Hell.

God's *wisdom* corresponds to what Aristotle called the "formal cause", the identity and intelligibility, which implies intelligence and design. God's *power* corresponds to what Aristotle called the "efficient cause", the ability to bring the effect into existence. God's *goodness* corresponds to what Aristotle called the "final cause", the end or value or purpose or goal. (See pensée 43.)

These correspond to the three divine attributes of the supreme God (Brahman) in Hinduism: *sat*, *chit*, and *ananda*. *Sat* is infinite being or life or power; *chit* is infinite wisdom or understanding or knowledge; and *ananda* is infinite joy or bliss or happiness, which comes only through love. (This is clearest in the bhakti kind of Hinduism.)

The final cause is the reason for the efficient cause's imposing the form or formal cause onto matter and the material cause and thus making the effect good and therefore joyful. Joy—our joy—is the ultimate reason, the final cause, for God's creating the universe. The Big Bang was for us! Did you think God cares more about galaxies than about persons? Maybe He would if He were a galaxy, but He's far greater than a gazillion galaxies (and so are we!)—He is three Persons.

48

The Simplest Secret of Joy

After thinking, reasoning, questioning, reading, philoso-
phizing, and theologizing for eighty-seven years (I'm a very
slow learner), I think I finally learned the single most simple
secret of joy. It's embarrassing how something so simple and
obvious could remain foggy and confused for so long. God
taught it to me, suddenly and surprisingly (not miraculously,
just by a nudge of intuition or inspiration), not on a spiritual
mountaintop but in a spiritual valley, when I feared falling into despair, failure, collapse, losing my reason, having
a nervous breakdown, or even becoming a Democrat. It
was Jesus' last words to us in Matthew's Gospel, a solemn,
God-guaranteed promise: "Behold, I am with you always."

He has not changed. He is "Jesus Christ ... the same
yesterday and today and for ever" (Heb 13:8). He is with
us now as surely as He was with His disciples and Peter
then, despite the fact that our Western culture, formerly
known as "Christendom", has apostasized. He comes to us
not from our culture but from Heaven.

The Good News trumps all Bad News. The Good
News is not just that He *did* rise but that He "*is* risen"
and is alive and kicking, here and now, and that we can
talk to Him all day, any day, because He is not deaf and
dumb. We can say Saint Faustina's simplest of all prayers,
"Jesus, I trust in You." We can ask Him, "Jesus, are You

with me? Are You with me now, in this?" We can pray that in the middle of any depression, temptation, loss, or misery. And we will always get an answer, even if we do not get an "experience" (which is usually a euphemism for a feeling). We *know* He hears and answers because that's what He promised us in the Gospel, and He always keeps His promises, unlike our modern heroes, politicians, and celebrities and even many of our parents.

That simple prayer is something we can pray whenever the Enemy attacks our bodies, psyches, minds, wills, or hearts—i.e., attacks us physically, emotionally, intellectually, morally, or spiritually. Even when we seem most passive and helpless, we can be active, we can choose, we can *do* something: we can offer up everything to Him who knows everything and controls everything and loves everything except our sins.

I know He is happy when I ask Him that question, "Jesus, are You with me?", especially in the middle of my sufferings and temptations to doubt. Blessed Fulton Sheen loved to say, "Don't waste your sufferings." They are where the most power is, like the trough of a wave. Knowing that and using it can begin to insert a strange but deep joy into our sorrows and pains.

The more we love, the more both our joys *and* our sorrows will be multiplied. The only way to avoid sorrows is to avoid love. Everyone and everything will break your heart if you give your heart away. Are you more concerned to avoid sorrow or to find joy? To flee the valleys or to climb the mountains? The only two places in this world where we can avoid all sorrows are the womb and the tomb. Between the two stands life, the great adventure. Jesus did not come to remove our adventures but to transform them.

49

The Joy of Purgatory and the Difference It Makes Now

One reason for the need for Purgatory is justice: both objective, impersonal, cosmic justice (the fact that both good and evil have necessary consequences, by their very nature) and perfect personal justice, for each of Heaven's citizens to be perfectly purified so that no evil can enter Heaven.

Justice is eternal and absolute because it is simply truth applied to moral good and evil. It is not only God's justice but also and above all His love that demands the pains of Purgatory, because those pains purge away all the dirt and defects in us that blind us and keep us from our joy—i.e., from fully seeing and enjoying God. As Christ said, it is only the pure of heart who can see God (Mt 5:8). All sins impair both our wisdom and our joy.

In Purgatory, we will understand this clearly, and therefore we will *will* the pains because we will see that they are the necessary pains of childbirth. The child to be born is our new self, our clean self, our true self. Our old self is its mother, and God is its Father. I think we will even have glimpses of the beautiful baby we are delivering.

This view of Purgatory casts transforming light on our pains *here*. Like those in Purgatory, they are willed by God's love for our joy. In this life, we need faith because we do not see, as God does, how they are necessary for our joy. But this faith is reasonable, as C. S. Lewis says in *A Grief Observed*: "The tortures occur. If they are unnecessary, then there is no God or a bad one. If there is a good God, then these tortures are necessary. For no even moderately good Being could possibly inflict or permit them if they weren't."[1]

Notice how stringently and tough-mindedly Lewis' argument appeals to reason! When we have faith, reason does not dim but brightens. After death it will be perfected: we will no longer need faith because we will see these truths and understand them with a terrible clarity, which will embrace both our terrible pain and our terrible joy. For we will be free from the limitations of earthly appearances and above all from our disordered and tempting passions and emotions (especially pride, lust, greed, and fear). Premodern saints typically saw the "blinding of the reason" as the worst of the effects of sin.

The great joy that Purgatory will make possible is that we will, finally, by God's grace, *merit* His just judgment: "Well done, good and faithful servant; ... enter into the joy of your master" (Mt 25:21). Grace (gift) and merit (deservingness), mercy and justice, will no longer be two contrasting things but will be identical.

---

[1] C. S. Lewis, *A Grief Observed* (New York: HarperOne, 1961), 43.

50

Joy Is Visible

When Jesus appeared to His disciples during the storm at sea, He was walking on the water, riding the waves as if they were horses. (Indeed, it is nearly impossible *not* to see certain foam-crested waves backlighted by sunlight without imagining galloping horses with flowing manes!)

When Jesus says to them, "It is I; do not be afraid" (Jn 6:20), He tells them three things.

First, He implies that we can see Him, who is our salvation and our joy and our deliverer from sin, suffering, death, and Hell. We can see Him by faith, though "through a glass, darkly" (1 Cor 13:12, KJV). Faith is not a work of our own imagination or opinion. Its object is truth, not in the abstract but in the One who said, "I am ... the truth" (Jn 14:6). Faith is a seeing, not a feeling.

Second, it is the fearsome storm that brings Him to us. He has tamed it, and He rides it like a cowboy. He is there, in it, on it, moving it. He is in the wind as well as the waves, and His Spirit is in their marriage. (In Tolkien's *Silmarillion*, Manwë, the god of the winds, and Ulmo, the god of the waters, are closest friends.)

Third, our fears, like the waves, can be ridden and conquered if we are in Him. He who made or allowed both storms, the inner fears and the outer waves, can also unmake them or disallow them.

Since Christ *is* our joy and since we can see Him by faith even in darkness and fear, we can find joy even there, not only in our sufferings but even in our fears, which His perfect providence is allowing to enter into our souls for now. He is really present in the storms as well as in the stilling. He is deliberately prolonging this storm, whatever it is, for a reason, and the reason is love. His reason for everything is love.

Miracles and divine providence are two ways this cause of our joy is visible, two clues that all things "work together for good" (Rom 8:28, KJV) even in this life. They are not proofs but only clues, signs, with "sign-ificance", that invite us to look along them, not just at them, to follow them like pointing fingers. There is enough light for those who seek and not so much light that it compels, against their will, those who do not will to seek, as does the light of the noonday sun. "Seek, and you will find" (Mt 7:7) implies also, "Don't seek and you won't find."

Thus, it is not necessity or luck or native intelligence that determines who finds God, truth, and heavenly joy and who does not. Instead, it is the heart's choice to seek and love the truth. For as Pascal said, "The heart has its reasons of which reason knows nothing."[1] The heart is deeper than both reason and feelings.

---

[1] Blaise Pascal, *Pensées*, trans. A. J. Krailsheimer (New York: Penguin Books, 1966), 127.

51

Living Purple or Living Beige

No one can choose joylessness over joy as such. We can choose only between true joy and false joy, between self-forgetful, self-giving love and the self-centered pursuit of personal pleasure or power or prestige—at which the heavens laugh in derision (Ps 2:4).

One form of false joy is beige: comfortable, safe, boring. Beige religion never produces either great saints *or* great sinners. (The Catholic Church has an abundance of both of those characters!) It is a flat life, a horizontal life, a safe life, a life without risk and adventure, without great sorrows or great joys. It is *nice*. It thinks what everyone thinks and values what everyone values and espouses only noncontroversial causes. No one is ever martyred for beige religion.

Purple religion is uncomfortable, controversial, and adventurous because it is risky and mysterious, both in its dogmas and its deeds. It produces spectacular saints and sinners. It lives in the heights and also in the depths. It is vertical, like a cathedral, not horizontal, like a modern ranch house. Both its joys and its sorrows are profound. It worships the wild and wonderful God who banged out the Big Bang and loved us pitiful jerks so much that He—well, you know the crazy extremes He went to in order to save us from sin and death and Hell (which, by the way, are three words that beige religion avoids) and get us into a Heaven of unimaginable, unspeakable, inconceivable, unlimited, unending ecstasy.

Purple has in it both red (fire) and blue (water), both volcanic lava and ocean waves. In Scripture, fire and water are symbols of both supernatural life and supernatural death. Beige is the color of desert sands, cat hair balls, and toddler diarrhea. Beige is not mentioned in Scripture because Scripture specializes in the strange, not the boring. Purple is. It is the costliest color, the color of kings and queens.

Jesus was not beige. He did not manage to unite His friends, who squabbled both then and now, but He did unite His enemies against Him, like Herod and Pilate, and the Pharisees and the Sadducees (Lk 23:12; Mt 16:1). He afflicted the comfortable and comforted the afflicted. He was not politically correct by the standards of His or any other time, including ours. He was not nice, but He was good. Like Aslan. Jesus was more like Aslan than Aslan is.

The happiness of the comfortable is beige. The happiness of the joyful is purple.

52

One More Time:
Joy, Sorrow, Suffering, and Love

There is no joy without love.

There is no love without sacrifice and suffering.

Reasoning from cause to effect: sacrifice and suffering, therefore love, therefore joy.

Reasoning from effect to cause: joy, therefore love, therefore sacrifice and suffering.

Love multiplies both our joys and our sufferings by the quantity of persons we love and by the quality and depth of our love for them.

God wants us to suffer because He wants us to learn to love, and He knows that nothing teaches us to love more than sacrifice.

God wants us to learn to love because He knows that nothing but love brings us the greatest joy.

That's purple religion. It's *formidable.*

We don't know how it works, how our simple intention to offer up to God all our joys and sufferings acquires somehow, by God's grace and our membership in His Mystical Body, the power to make a real difference for good for both ourselves and those we love, a difference that, if we saw it now as we shall see it in Heaven, would paralyze us with responsibility. We don't know how God works these physical and emotional evils out for good, but only that He does. And we know also, if we dare to listen to reason, that the only alternative to trusting God's wisdom and authority is not trusting it, which means trusting our own wisdom and authority to judge it—which, in turn, means denying the two most basic truths in the world: that God is God and that we are not.

53

The Way to Joy Is and
Is Not Rocket Science

The way to joy is rocket science because it turns our souls into rockets, flaming gloriously through the darkness of space into the heavens.

It is not rocket science because it is very simple. (That's exactly why it's so rare and difficult for us.) The road to joy was well known to all honest and thoughtful people throughout human history, but it is not to our contemporary culture's prophets, the pop psychologists. The first step on the road is to stop being so self-centered! Stop whining. Stop thinking of yourself as a victim. The universe is not about you. Life is not about you. Even *you* are not about you. You are about God and His other kids, your spiritual siblings, your "neighbors".

So stop using those stupid, shallow, selfish, whiny victim terms, such as "microaggressions" and "trigger warnings". Grow a spine and a thick skin. Forget yourself. If you don't learn to do that now, you'll never be able to do it in Heaven after you die except after a long and painful Purgatory. If you went to Heaven in your present condition, you wouldn't feel at home there, because all those in Heaven forget themselves there. That's why they are in joy. They don't try to cram joy into themselves; they enter a joy that is not just bigger than themselves but *terribly* bigger.

Every religion in the world knows some aspect of the great secret that the self lives only when it dies. Even outside religion, people know that by experience. Whether God exists or not, you're not Him. You're not the center of reality. The sun does not rise each morning because you wake up. You wake up because the sun rises. And after death, you will wake up because the Son rises.

So please stop listening to the ridiculous lie that "you can be whatever you want to be", the lie that our commencement speakers tell us. Your name is not Jesus; you are not going to save the world. And the world is certainly not going to save you. If you want to know who will, look at the image that's banned from our politics, our education, our polite conversation, and our media. It's the image of a man being tortured to death on a cross. Incredibly, but truly, He is the one who is the secret of your joy.

That's really all I need to say. It's all there.

54

Is It Selfish to Seek Our Own Joy?

Is it selfish to seek our own joy? No. Self-love is not in itself evil. We are implicitly commanded to love ourselves when we are commanded to love our neighbors *as ourselves*. So our innate drive for joy, for ourselves as well as for those we love, is precious. It is our divine discontent, our Augustinian "restless heart". To seek sorrow rather than joy deliberately is unnatural and pathological.

One thing that makes our search for joy unselfish is that the joy we are to search for cannot be selfishly *possessed* because it is much bigger than we are. We enter it rather than it entering us. (See pensée 24.) It is the joy of God, the very life of God.

The fact that this joy of God is love (*agape*) is a second reason it is unselfish. Joy is simply the smell of love, the taste of love, the color of love, the inevitable effect of love.

A third reason the search for joy is not selfish is that our absolute is God and His will, not our own. God cannot be used as a means because He is the final end. Nor should other persons be used merely as means, since they are made in God's image. If they are Christians, they have His very life in them.

Fourth, joy is not itself our end because it is only the smell of the food, not the food; not the supreme good itself but only the experience of possessing it, or the presence of it. God is that "it", Absolute Good.

Fifth, true love, and thus the true joy that is its fruit, is self-forgetful. In contrast, "Oh look! I am now doing God's will! I am being sanctified!" or "I am having a religious experience!"—that is self-destructive, for as soon as we attend to ourselves having this self-forgetful experience, it ceases to be self-forgetful and thus ceases to be itself. In fact, it becomes proud and thus joyless. For remember, joy is a cat, not a dog. (See pensée 13.) This is true even of happiness, pleasure, and health. Hypochondriacs worry themselves sick.

The greater a thing is, the more the danger of making it into an idol. Don't do that with joy. God is joy, but joy is not God.

Don't do that with love either. Love as a principle is only an abstraction; love's object, God, is not an abstraction but a Person. God is love, but love is not God.

("A is B" or "A is not B" means something very different from "A equals B" or "A does not equal B." Equations are reversible because their two sides are equal. Sentences are not. The subject of a sentence is the topic; the predicate is the speech or the sermon or the article. The subject is the title; the predicate is the book. The subject is something the speaker or writer assumes is known by the listener or the reader; the predicate is information that the speaker or writer thinks will be new or controversial or surprising to the listener or reader. "God is love" means "Let me tell you something remarkable about the God you already know: He is love, simply love, total love, all the way through." "Love is God" means "Let me tell you something about the love you already know. It is God, it is the absolute, it is what you must worship; seek no further.")

55

Christ or Joy?

If Christ is the Lord of your life, answer this question: You know that Christ is the source of your joy, both now and in Heaven; but what if Christ offered you the choice between Himself without joy or joy without Himself. Which do you choose?

If you are sincere when you offer God all your joys and sufferings of this day, the answer is clear. We all love joy and hate suffering, and we also love God and hate evil, but our love of God and goodness must trump our love of joy, and our hate for evil must trump our hate for sorrow and suffering. Thus, "Your will be done" is our absolute, not "joy be done." If Christ comes to you with His cross rather than His crown, there are only two options: you accept both, or you accept neither. There is no third option, no crossless Christ.

Indeed, Christ brings us resurrection joy as well as suffering and death; the crown as well as the cross; the glory as well as the gory. But it is equally true that Christ brings us the cross as well as the crown. Why? Because we have to cross out ourselves in order to make a place for Him in our hearts, in the very center of our being. We need a heart transplant. And we can't have two hearts. The old one has to go to make room for the new one that God wants to create (Ps 51:10). And we add to the pain by struggling against that operation; that is why we have to die: death is like anesthesia.

That means that life is the beginning of Purgatory. But Purgatory is the beginning of Heaven, not of Hell. The cross leads to the crown. The Sorrowful Mysteries lead to the Glorious Mysteries. The death of "our former man", the unholy, fallen "flesh", leads to the birth of the New Man, the man enlivened by the Holy Spirit (Rom 6:6; 7:5–6). ("The flesh" in Scripture refers not to the body but to the sinful soul. The soul's spiritual death, or separation from God by sin, is the cause of the body's physical death. The body is the victim, not the villain.)

No one knows why God gives some people more joys and others less, why some get more sufferings and others less. "God only knows." That's His answer to Job's question "Why me?" (To answer the most important questions, it's not what you know; it's who you know that counts most.) Often, God comes to us without the joy that always follows eventually in His wake. Sometimes this lack of joy lasts a day, sometimes months, sometimes nearly a lifetime, as it did with Mother Teresa's "dark night of the soul". But joy follows God as surely as three angles follow a triangle.

Meanwhile, we do not love Christ because He gives us joy. We love Christ because He gives us God.

56

What Causes the Greatest Joy?

What causes the greatest joy? Loving and being loved.

The greatest loving subject is God, and the most lovable object is God. Therefore, the completest joy comes from loving God completely (when we are the subjects and God is the object) and knowing how God loves us completely (when we are the objects and God is the subject).

How do we know how completely God loves us? Look at a crucifix. That's how much.

If Christ could have redeemed the world with a single drop of His divine blood at His circumcision, why did He pour out all ten pints of His blood on the cross? Because He had ten pints to give. That's what complete love does: it gives everything. The surest measure of love is suffering and sacrifice.

When Jesus was crucified, He stretched out His arms to show us how much He loves us: infinitely, without limit. The arms of God's love extend beyond the finite bounds of the universe. A circle has a limit, a circumference; a cross can extend its four arms to infinity.

But the joy of love and the suffering of love are a package deal. They cannot be separated. They meet on the cross.

Where is there the most love? Where there is the most suffering and sacrifice. This is true both of God's love to us and of our love to God and one another. God's gift to us of the privilege of suffering for Him is His deepest love, His deepest sword thrust into our hearts, His deepest heart surgery. And it calls forth our deepest faith in and love for God. We all know from experience how much we tend to forget Him and take Him for granted in normal times, but we are driven toward Him more deeply the more deeply we suffer, as we appreciate a life preserver the most when our boat sinks.

The next time you feel like crying a large river, remember that fact: that suffering, accepted in faith, powerfully unites us to God. Whether you feel that or not, whether that comforts you or not, you know that it is true; you know that it is real; you know that it is there; you know that *He* is there, working there, working on you, working all things together, especially your sorrows, for your greater joy. "Blessed are those who mourn, for they shall be comforted" (Mt 5:4).

57

Why Is "How Do We Get This Joy?" a Trick Question?

How do we get Christ's joy? It's really a trick question. If we are Christians, the answer is this: in the same way we get two eyes and one mouth. We already have joy if we have Christ, whether we know it or not and whether we feel it or not. We don't get to Him; He gets to us.

And how does He get to us? In many ways. The first one is through faith and Baptism, which are always joined in Scripture. The way of His getting to us that seems the most joyful and the most total is through mystical experiences. But He gives these foretastes of Heaven rarely and to only a few. There is another gift that He gives to all His children, not just to a few, and although it does not usually "taste" like the mystical "foretaste" of Heaven, it is, in objective fact, an intimacy, a closeness, and a union that surpasses even the most mystical of mystical experiences and is the most complete and perfect union with God that is possible to anyone in this life. I received that gift this very morning.

It is, of course, Holy Communion. In it, the whole of God enters into the whole of us. It is the whole of God because Christ is the whole of God, not a part of God; and it is the whole of us because He enters both our bodies

and our souls. We receive His divinity with His humanity because, in Him, divinity is one with humanity. We
receive His soul with His body because His soul is one
with His body. We receive His blood and His flesh separately because His blood and His flesh were separated in
death. But that is a "more" rather than a "less" because it
means that we receive His death as well as His life.

Surely this is a miracle absolutely impossible for any
human mind ever to have guessed. "What no eye has seen,
nor ear heard, nor the heart of man conceived, what God
has prepared for those who love him" (1 Cor 2:9): that is
usually, and rightly, applied to the joys of Heaven, but it
applies as literally to the Eucharist.

The Eucharist is a fuller union with God and a greater
joy than any mystical experience, even though we do not
usually feel it. Feelings are only its effects, its spillover, its
taste and smell, its touch and feel. Feelings are not it but
only what it feels like. As Saint Thomas Aquinas says in his
Adoro Te Devote, "Sight, touch, and taste in Thee are each
deceived; / The ear alone most safely is believed: / I believe
all the Son of God has spoken, / Than Truth's own word
there is no truer token."

God gives many gifts to us, but the greatest is Himself.
In the Eucharist, the Gift is the Giver. He cannot give anything more because there is, in all reality and possibility,
nothing more than that Giver. In the Eucharist, He gives
His whole self to our whole self and comes closer, with
more withness, more oneness, more union than is possible
or conceivable.

58

Joy for Christ or Christ for Joy?

The more important a point is, the more we need to repeat it. Jesus did not condemn repetition; in fact, He gave us only one prayer, which He obviously meant for us to repeat many, many times. No lover ever sighs, "Oh no, not the same words again" when he hears the magic words "I love you." But we all have serious spiritual attention deficit disorder, whether it's hyperactive or inattentive or both. We need repetition.

In the Morning Offering, we offer all our joys to God. What does that mean? I think it means spiritually the same thing it means physically whenever we give anyone a gift: detachment and sacrifice. Detachment from our hands, sacrifice of our ownership of it. We want to give God "the good gift" (the literal meaning of "Eucharist") of our whole selves, of everything we have, in a grateful response to His giving us His whole self, everything He has, His very life, both His incarnate human life, on the cross, and His divine life, in which He invites us to participate ("theosis", 2 Pet 1:4). We can do this perfectly only in the Mass, in the Eucharist.

We all want joy and not suffering, so when we offer both our joys and our sufferings to God, we are exchanging our will for His will, saying to Him, "Your will be done, whether it is joy or suffering. My will is joy, but if what You will for me now is not to feel subjectively the joy I really objectively have because I have You, then Your will be done. Because I sacrifice my will to Your will, I sacrifice the joy I want for the suffering You want for me. My will is not to suffer, but if You will me to suffer, Your will, not mine, be done. You are my absolute—nothing else, not even joy. You are my joy; joy is not my God."

God forces us to make this hard choice when He comes to us in suffering, which is relatively rare. Almost all of us have many more joys than sufferings, and suffering is always temporary, whether it is short or long. For joy, like truth, is God's property, not His accident. Our suffering is the accident masking the real presence of joy, like the accidents of bread and wine in the Eucharist. Behind the appearance is the reality, the real presence.

Christ is both our joy and our suffering, both our crown and our cross. Would we rather have Christ or joy? We want both; we want a crossless Christ; but there is no such thing. There are many Christless crosses but no crossless Christ. Indeed, Christ brings us resurrection as well as death, crown as well as cross, glory as well as humiliation, Heaven's banquet room as well as Heaven's bathroom, which is Purgatory and suffering and sacrifice and discipline and reparation. But Purgatory brings us to Heaven, not to Hell.

Joy does not give us God; God gives us joy—the same God who gives us suffering. When we suffer, we not only suffer *with* Christ, but we also suffer *Christ*; we receive Christ, as the body on the operating table suffers the cut of the surgeon's knife, receives the knife. Suffering, for a Christian, is not like a test from a remote and stern teacher; it is more like the reception of Holy Communion.

59

Joy's Eschatology

One of the reasons why we lack joy today, why we do not have the lively faith, hope, and love of Heaven that our poor and primitive ancestors had, is that we are rich and sophisticated, not poor and primitive. Where they saw gold and glory when they peered ahead on life's road, we see only emptiness and fogginess. They had the theological virtue of hope in a more substantial and certain way than we do. They were not puzzled or surprised at the words of the Catholic burial liturgy, "the *sure and certain* hope of the resurrection" (emphasis added). Those "traditionalists" or "conservatives" or "primitives" were more radically "progressive" than we are. For a conservative, by definition, is someone who focuses on conserving the goods he already has, while the progressive, by definition, wants to progress to goods he does not yet have. To think that seeking the goods we do not have is more important than enjoying the goods we do have is a very strange and joyless philosophy.

Surely, the reason God gives us sufferings and losses is not only to teach us detachment from earthly goods that we can idolize and become addicted to but also to encourage and inflame our hope for heavenly joy—a hope that is also a joy in itself, as the anticipation of a great banquet is part of the joy of the banquet, and as spiritual or physical foreplay is part of spiritual or physical lovemaking. There is more joy in going to Jerusalem on a donkey than in going in circles on a luxurious cruise ship.

Aron Nimzowitsch, one of the best chess players in the world in the 1920s, said, "The threat is stronger than its execution."[1] His point was that sometimes the fear of evil does more harm (to the loser) than the evil feared. That's true of many earthly evils and miseries, such as defeat in chess or war. The positive converse of this negative principle is also often true of earthly goods and joys: that it is better to travel hopefully than to arrive. That can't be true of everything, for then there would be nothing to hope for! But it is true of many things. Arrival is often disappointing. Success is often a bummer. But God is never disappointing. And thus, the anticipation of Heaven can be part of its joy. As Saint Teresa of Avila reputedly said, "All the way to Heaven is Heaven." Even Purgatory is part of Heaven. That's why its joys are greater than any earthly joys. (See pensée 49.)

---

[1] Quoted in Yasser Seirawan, introduction to *My System: 21st Century Edition*, by Aron Nimzowitsch, ed. Lou Hays (Dallas: Hays Publishing, 1991), i.

60

How *Sobornost* Magnifies Joy

Sobornost, often translated "universality", is a Russian word for the principle that because humanity is a single body, a family, everything everyone in this family does affects everyone else in the family, for good or for evil. There are no victimless crimes. Because the whole human race is one family, and doubly because the Mystical Body of Christ, the Church, is one family, everyone affects everyone else. This organic unity is mirrored by the physical unity of the universe, the uni (one) versa (diversity). Every particle of matter makes a difference to every other by universal gravitation. Gravity is love on the merely physical level, and the aim of love is unity. These universal gravity waves in the universe, and the universal moral and spiritual waves in the human universe, are not separate and independent particles, even though people, like the photons of light, are individuals. The universe, like light, is both wave and particle, both continuous and discontinuous, both one and many.

Sobornost is spiritual gravity waves, waves of love or hate, good or evil. Everything makes a difference to everything else in some way, both physically and spiritually. The simplest good deed or prayer from your hands or lips today may make the difference between despair and hope in the life of someone a hundred years from now. It may be the straw that breaks the camel's back or the vote that wins the election. Why should spirit be less richly, invisibly, subtly, and universally related and interdependent than matter?

If we love our neighbor, one of our greatest joys is that we can actually give him greater joy by the deeds of love that we do. We usually confine this to visible deeds, but *sobornost* vastly increases the power of love to cause joy to both the doer and the recipient, by the insight that all of humanity is the recipient—and perhaps even more than humanity. For Dostoyevsky's Father Zossima in *The Brothers Karamazov*, even the birds would be happier if we were holier. Deeds of love are like pebbles thrown into pools: the rings of force keep moving outward and affecting more and more of the pool, as light from the sun fills the whole space-pool of the universe, since it would be observable even from distant galaxies if we had sufficient magnification. Someone on a planet two thousand light-years from Earth could see Jesus Christ living and dying in Israel, because those light waves are still there two thousand years later in time and two thousand light-years away in space. The light from deeds, the intelligibility of deeds, does not die; it expands into the entire universe in the form of light.

As Saint Anselm teaches (see pensée 24), everyone's joy in Heaven is multiplied by the number of others that person loves, because love rejoices as much in the beloved's joy as in that of oneself. *Sobornost* multiplies that multiplication.

This physical analogy fulfills Aquinas' description of joy as "effulgent". He says that goodness, by its very nature, is diffusive of itself. Jacques Maritain speaks of a universal "ontological generosity". Everything makes a difference to everything else.

Sobornost transcends not only the limitations of individuality but also the different levels in man: the spiritual joy of holiness increases the psychological joy of happiness, and happiness increases the body's health. Happy people live longer. Infinitely happy people live forever.

61

How Does It All Work?

How does God's providence work? How does love work? How does *sobornost* work? How do justification and sanctification and glorification work? What's the mechanism and the method?

The first answer is that there is no mechanism or method, because it's not a machine. God created all the matter/energy in the whole universe at once in the Big Bang, and the only means or method or mechanism He used was Himself, His Word, who said, "Be!"

The second answer is that we don't need to know how things work in order to use them and enjoy them. We don't have to know the physics of electricity to put the lights on; all we need to know is the command: "Flip the switch." We don't need to know how chemistry works to know that after thunderstorms or when we're near waterfalls or breaking waves we feel more alert and alive. (It's the negative ions that do it.) All we need to know is that it does work and where to go to enjoy it. And we don't need to know the "spiritual technology" of divine providence in order to know what we do, in fact, know—namely, that we find joy when, and to the extent that, we stop seeking our own joy and start seeking that of others and when we stop insisting "My will be done" and instead pray and mean (and live) "Thy will be done." We don't have to *explain* the paradox of life through death, getting through giving, glory through humility; we just have to *live* it. At the Last Judgment, we will be evaluated not on the clarity in our heads but on the charity in our hearts.

But the divine "joy strategy" doesn't *always* work because it works through us, and we are stupid, selfish, shallow sinners and fumbling fools. That's why not all suffering brings us closer to God and (eventually) greater joy, but only the sufferings that are accepted in faith and offered up in hope and love. When we plunge our sufferings into the "transformation machine" of Christ, they are transformed into joy, as His death-getting is transformed into life-giving. In other words, the only "how" that we need to know, the only "mechanism" or means that makes the difference between joy and misery, is our own choices. God is "single-minded": He wants good only. We are not single-minded but double-minded. We are the only clog in the joy machine.

And we know this not just by supernatural faith but also by repeated natural experience. In fact, it takes supernatural effort on the part of the Devil to make us ignore or forget this experiential data, this simple fact.

The laboratory of life is a great teacher. That is part of God's design. The results of endlessly repeated experiments are consistent, realistic, and relatable: whenever we will "My will be done", we are eventually disappointed, and whenever we will "Thy will be done", we are surprised by joy, always deep down and in the long run and usually even at the moment that we give up our wills to God's. This is not ideologically imposed on experience but confirmed by experience.

But since God is the Father, not the Godfather, He makes us an offer we can refuse instead of making us an offer we can't refuse. When we refuse it, we always find misery, and when we accept it, we always find joy. Yet we keep refusing. We are quite insane. Our only hope is the amazing fact that our Father's love for His children is even crazier than we are. Nothing explains love; love explains everything.

62

Joy in Old Age?

I am a pessimist by temperament and an optimist by conviction—i.e., by faith. My human nature is cynical and prone to despair. It tells me, among other things, that "the golden years" are a scam. Here is the argument of my temperament. We die either young and unexpectedly or old and expectedly—i.e., after an extended period of decline and decay. There is sorrow, not joy, either way. The concept of "a happy death" makes sense only in terms of the hope of Heaven, not in terms of our medical, emotional, and mental condition here in this world. Joy seems to be entropic, like life itself. Only when we ignore this fact can we experience present joys without noticing the ghostly prophet of inevitable death grinning at us from behind the flowers. So joy comes only at the expense of truth, at least in this world.

My answer to myself does not deny the data. Of course we all have to suffer death, which is the total loss of all earthly joys, whether death is sudden or gradual. In both cases, our joy decreases, whether suddenly or gradually. That is all true, but it is not the whole truth. For the hope of eternal joy gives us a greater joy here and now in this vale of tears, this valley of the shadow of death.

Two men are walking to London: one to be crowned king and one to be beheaded. The path and the number of steps to be taken by the two men are the same. Yet the different destinations make every step different. If that seems an extreme claim, ask yourself this question: Would you exchange the hope of eternal heavenly joy for more temporal earthly joy, even if you could have all the temporal joys that you wanted but without the hope of Heaven? Would you give up infinity for the finite?

The pessimist sees something true. He looks ahead and notices that the future (dying and death) casts a dark shadow on the present. But the hope-filled person looks further ahead and notices that the further future (Heaven) casts a light even on that dark shadow. This world is indeed "the valley of the shadow of death", yet in it we are able to say, "I fear no evil; for you are with me" (Ps 23:4). We say that not to ourselves but to God. We can actually talk to the Light that conquers the darkness.

But the pessimist has a precious point, a timely truth: that in the end, either God or death has the last word. If we have no hope in God and Heaven, we have no hope at all, in the end. It's God or nothing. That's true for everyone, no matter how joy-filled or joy-empty one's life may be. The difference between hope and hopelessness is far greater than the difference between tiny joy and enormous joy. It is the difference between Heaven and Hell.

Other religions know God much less well, for they do not know Christ. Yet they know Him a little, for they, too, hope for Something More, however inadequately understood. If God equals one million, and the number for how much other religions know Him is only four, what is ours? Is it more like eight hundred thousand or more like eight?

63

Is It Really God or Nothing?
No Joy apart from God?

We can see most clearly that it is indeed "God or nothing" (in the words of the title of Cardinal Sarah's book) when we confront the death of someone we love.

Esther Maria Magnis knew this. This is what she discovered when her father died: that nothing, absolutely nothing, seemed to remain. Her entire world collapsed. Her father had been the center of her world and her life. But neither he nor she believed in God. She discovered by experience that "there is no hope without God. I looked for it for four years. It doesn't exist."[1]

That is the profound truth that pessimism and nihilism and despair teach us. But it is not the whole truth. For later, when Esther's younger brother died at the age of twenty-three, "his faith in God was so great that it carried us all with him. He was not afraid. There was a peace in his prayers that I don't understand.... It was like the love I had and still have for him and for my father. A love that won't let me go, and won't die, and seems ... otherworldly."[2]

---

[1] Esther Maria Magnis, "The Strange Love of a Strange God", trans. Chris Zimmerman, *Plough Quarterly*, no. 31 (March 18, 2022), https://www.plough .com/en/topics/life/grieving/the-strange-love-of-a-strange-god.
[2] Ibid.

It *is* otherworldly, because it's *God*. Love is what God does because it's what God is.

If you don't believe God loves you, you have no hope. If you have no hope, you have no joy. If you have no joy, you have nothing, no matter how much else you have. So it is truly God or nothing.

64

How Can We Have Joy in Heaven
If Someone We Love Is in Hell?

Suppose that when you get to Heaven, you discover that someone you loved with all your heart (a spouse, a child, a parent) died without faith or Baptism and was in Hell. How could you accept or enjoy Heaven?

Are you content because you no longer love that person? How could you love less rather than more in Heaven?

Is it because you forget that loved one is in Hell? How could heavenly joy depend on ignorance? Must not true joy be based on truth?

That is not an easy question to answer, and we do not have a definitive answer to it. But we have good guesses, clues, probabilities, and analogies.

For one thing, God solves it in Himself, somehow. His joy cannot be held hostage to our misery. But He cannot compromise either His love or His truth. If He can solve this problem, He can share His solution with us. This is true even if we do not now know *how* He does it. But we know that His love, His power, and His wisdom are far greater than ours.

There is a good guess about how He does it, and how we will do it, in the distinction between passive love and active love. God does not "fall in love" any more than the ocean falls into water. His lack of passive emotions is not a lack at all but an overplus. He *is* love, so He cannot fall in love. He continues to love all those in Hell without His joy being held hostage to theirs. They cannot have the power to veto His joy.

And even though we cannot experience or imagine our emotions being purely active, as God's are, we can experience the distinction between passive love and active love. When someone we love does something self-destructive, it makes us sad and angry, and we say, "How could you do that stupid thing?" We mean two things: "How could you do it to yourself? How could you make yourself so miserable?" and "How could you do that to me? How could you make me so miserable?" I think in Heaven we will still love in the first way but not in the second. We will no longer suffer, passively, but we will not cease to love, actively.

Or perhaps we will continue to mourn over those loved ones, but the mourning will be purely active and a joy. As Gandalf says at the parting of the Hobbits at the end of *The Lord of the Rings*, "Not all tears are an evil." That any persons are in Hell cannot be a pure joy to anyone who loves them, but perhaps there is a joy in pure, heavenly sorrow—a joy that we barely comprehend. For even here, joy can be found in sorrow, so that the very sorrow can be a joy, although joy cannot itself be a sorrow. Marian apparitions and statues often weep, so perhaps in Heaven there are good tears, which God wipes away (Rev 21:4).

We're not sure how it works, but we are sure that joy must trump sorrow. Somehow, the blessed in Heaven can tolerate the sorrows of the damned, although the damned cannot tolerate the joys of the blessed. For joy does not depend on sorrow but sorrow depends on joy, as love does not depend on hate but hate depends on love: we hate only what destroys or removes or harms what we love.

All this is only a guess and a clue, not a certainty. Perhaps we cannot imagine any of these solutions. But God can. And the differences between this life and the next are probably much greater than we can imagine.

65

Joy and Sorrow in the Rosary

The Rosary's biggest lesson is too big for us to notice, like the names of the continents on maps when we focus on the details and overlook the "big picture".

There are four continents in the Rosary, only one for sorrow (the Sorrowful Mysteries) and three for joy (the Joyful Mysteries, the Luminous Mysteries, and the Glorious Mysteries).

When we are "in" any one of these four continents, we should not forget the even bigger picture of all four together in one real world, one story, one history. Our joys in this world will always alternate with sorrows, but even here, there are always more things to be joyful about than there are things to be sorrowful about on the whole, even though we feel our small sorrows more keenly than we feel our larger joys.

Similarly, Aquinas says that even though we feel hate (and most other evils) more keenly than we feel love (and most other goods), hatred can never be stronger than love because an effect can never be stronger than its cause; and some love, the love of some thing, is always the cause of our hate, since nothing is hated except because it is contrary to something that is loved.[1] The lesson here is that our feelings are a very unreliable index of reality.

[1] *ST* I-II, q. 29, arts. 2, 3.

There is sorrow even in the Joyful Mysteries, e.g., Simeon's prophecy to Mary that "a sword will pierce through your own soul" in the Presentation of the Child Jesus in the Temple (Lk 2:35). But there is also joy even in the Sorrowful Mysteries because they are the cause of our hope of Heaven; and the death of Christ on the cross is really the death of death. John Donne spoke God's own word to Death when he wrote in "Death, Be Not Proud", "Death, thou shalt die."

The Rosary begins and ends in joy. Our life, too, began not in sorrow but in rejoicing, at birth. When you were born, everyone else was smiling; you were the only one screaming in protest! And at the end of our lives in this world, our sorrows will turn into joys and even glories, like Christ's.

The happy ending of deliverance presupposes some evil we are delivered from. The greater the evil, the greater the joy of the deliverance from it. We get foretastes of that joy and glory even now, in great stories and great lives, when tears of joy follow tears of sorrow. They are appetizers of Heaven.

66

Some of the Heavenly Appetizers
of Joy and Glory

What are some of those appetizers of Heaven that we know in this world?

We know them in the magic words of the poets.

We know them in the wordless word of great music, work of the Muses, not of man.

We know them in the word spoken by human love, the moment when the world's most prosaic word suddenly becomes the most wonder-full word in the world, the word "we".

We know them in a High Mass in a great cathedral, in the solemn joy of adoration before the astonishing mystery of God-with-us, when we are side by side with Mary, hailed by the angelic annunciation of the heavenly glory, visited from another world, another dimension.

We know them in great art, when a picture becomes no longer an object *in* this world but a magic window opening up to another world for us, a hole in our world, as the stars were to the ancient Greeks and as the painting of the *Dawn Treader* was to the Pevensie children.

We know them in the electric shock of an absolutely perfect flower, or in the clear crystal glass of a winter night, or in the seagull's haunting call to return to Mother Sea.

For some, the glory is not so much in the far country as in the magic word "home", the fairest place on earth, attained after Ulyssean adventures, Herculean labors, or prodigal wanderings aplenty.

We will all know it flat in the face when we die, when we shall be hailed by the Angel of Death with the same lightsome glory with which Mary was hailed by the Angel of Life, because Christ has made Death into life's golden chariot, sent to fetch us, His Cinderella Bride, out of the cinders of this ashpit of a world, through a far midnight ride, to His very own castle and bedchamber, where Glory will beget glory upon us forever.[1]

(Forgive me for quoting myself. It was inspired by C. S. Lewis' golden sermon "The Weight of Glory".)

---

[1] Peter Kreeft, *Heaven: The Heart's Deepest Longing* (San Francisco: Ignatius Press, 2013), 233–34.

67

Does God Change His Love toward Us When We Change Ours toward Him?

God's love toward us never changes, even when our love toward Him does. Look at the analogy of the sun. Like the light of the sun, the light of the Son does not change from good to evil when it burns us. That burning happens only because we are foolish enough to face it without mediation or because we *need* the burning to correct our sinful habits and addictions or to move us on to greater joy through the sufferings of that joyless time.

We seem to experience the sun changing from our friend to our enemy when we experience too much or too little of its heat. But that is an illusion of perspective, a projection of *our* change onto the sun—and also onto the Son of God, who never changes His loving will toward us, even when we change ours toward Him, who never relaxes the light (truth) and heat (love) that are Himself. He is "Jesus Christ ... the same yesterday and today and for ever" (Heb 13:8). But His effects in us change because we change.

We do not experience the fact that Christ is unchangeable. We know it by faith. In that faith is our joy. When that faith is greater than a mustard seed, it can move mountains.

Our joy is not unchanging, but the cause and object and reason of our joy is the unchanging and unchangeable nature of God's love for us. At every moment, God fills us with as much of His joy as we can take, as our limitations of mind and will allow to come through, just as the sun gives us as much light and heat as the clouds will let through the earth's atmosphere.

For, as Saint Thomas said, "whatever is received, is always received according to the mode (and degree) of the receiver."[1] No finite soul can ever receive *all* of God's infinite love and light. God sculpts our souls to hollow out larger places in them to contain larger portions of His love and thus His joy. (For love, remember, is not a feeling inside the lover; it is a real entity, like gravity, that goes out of the lover and into the beloved. Its category is neither "substance" nor "accident" but "relationship".) This sculpting process is often painful, of course; yet the need and reason for it, and God's only motive for it, is our own greater joy. If He left the option up to us, we would all choose lesser sculpting, thus lesser suffering but also lesser perfection, lesser love, and lesser joy in the end. For those in a state of grace, sufferings are not God's punishments for our sins (although we need them because of our sins) but strokes of love from an Artist sculpting a masterpiece. They are not spankings but kisses.

[1] *ST* I, q. 75, art. 5.

68

Love Times *X* Equals Joy. What Is *X*?

Love multiplies joy in two ways and also by two factors. The two ways are that when you experience joy, you want to share it with those you love so that your joy multiplies their joy; and when you see someone you love experiencing joy, their joy multiplies yours. The two factors that multiply joy are quality and quantity: the quality or depth or passion of your love and the quantity of persons you love.

There is one form of love that cannot be increased in quantity: in marriage, you give your whole self to *one* other person. If you try to give your whole self to more than one person, you will not find yourself, your love, and your joy multiplied. You will find it divided.

Love multiplies not only joy but also sorrow and suffering in these same two ways and by these same two qualitative and quantitative multipliers. When those you love suffer, you suffer too, and when you suffer, you make those who love you suffer too. And the more deeply in quality and the more extensively in quantity you love, the more you suffer.

When others suffer, you suffer *for* them and *with* them and even *in* them. For love makes you suffer *for* them as their lovers and servants, and puts you *with* them as a "we", and even *in* them as they become part of your identity.

(Your love changes your identity as much as your identity changes your love.)

For love unites two people without confusing them, since it unites their goods and their evils, their joys and their sufferings, but not their substance. Thus, even human love, if it is *agape*, is an image of the unique unity of the Persons of the Trinity, which Saint Bernard of Clairvaux defines as "total harmony of wills without confusion of substances".[1]

This suffering for and with and in others is much greater if you cannot relieve their sufferings. You would gladly exchange places with them, but you cannot, and that adds to your suffering. Perhaps the worst suffering of all is seeing someone you love not just suffering but suffering because of his own follies and bad choices. Or because of yours, since that adds the suffering of guilt. Your suffering is even worse if he rebuffs your efforts to help him to get free and to undo his self-destructive choices. It is worst of all if the more you try to help him, the more he feels threatened by you. He feels you are his enemy, trying to control him. How Christ must suffer in His human nature when we do this to Him!

The commonest example of this most sorrowful of sufferings is to be the parent of a self-destructive child, such as Saint Monica to Saint Augustine. The only greater suffering is to be the divine Parent of *us* self-destructive children. For all sin is self-destructive. Jesus' worst suffering was not feeling the tortures in His body but seeing the spiritual misery in the souls of His torturers, seeing the satanic joy in their sadism, knowing where it came from, and knowing where it must lead them to. His only mitigation of that sorrow

---

[1] Quoted in Étienne Gilson, *History of Christian Philosophy in the Middle Ages* (Washington, D.C.: Catholic University of America Press, 2019), 165.

was the hope that they could be forgiven "for they know not what they do" (Lk 23:34). I suspect that His greatest suffering was not on the cross but in Gethsemane if, at that time, Satan showed Him all His beloved children in Hell in his clutches, despite Christ's saving work. That would have caused Him to bleed more painfully than the cross did.

69

Buddha's Salvation from Suffering— and from Joy

Buddha knew suffering well enough to know it was the one common factor in all of life. His "first noble truth" is "To live is to suffer" (*dukkha*). Christ saves us from sin; Buddha saves us from suffering.

And Buddha knew that personal, wholehearted love multiplies our sufferings. So, like the Stoics, he advised us not to love *or* hate anyone actively. He believed that love is a personal investment and if we invest our joy in others by loving them personally, we become their hostages. If we give our hearts away, they will certainly be broken. So the "second noble truth" is that the cause of suffering is desire: *eros* in Greek, *tanha* in Sanskrit. It means desire for something for oneself, for some pleasure; to be pleased. There is no word in Sanskrit like *agape* for *unselfish* desire, a different kind of personal love that contrasts with *eros*. The Buddhist word for the contrast with *tanha* is *karuna*, which is not a personal desire, emotion, or will but a kind of mental but not emotional empathy, an impersonal consciousness of identity with the sufferer. Individuality is an illusion for Buddha. He says there is no *atman*, or "deep self", any more than there is any *jiva*, or ego-self. What we call "persons" are only "strands" (*skandhas*) of impersonal consciousness that fate knotted at birth.

Since desire (*eros, tanha*) is the cause of suffering and since the way to remove an effect is to remove its cause, it follows that the removal of desire is the way to the removal of suffering. Buddha's "third noble truth" is that this can be done, that all suffering can be "extinguished" (that is the meaning of "Nirvana").

And Buddha's "fourth noble truth" is that it is done by the "noble eightfold path" of ending desires, both loves and hates, in all eight areas of life that he distinguishes, both inner and outer.

Buddha is a "savior" from suffering, not from sin. He has no concept of sin as a broken relationship with God. Though his "salvation" may be the way to Nirvana, it is not the way to Heaven or to joy. Buddha was a great psychologist, but he misdiagnosed the disease that removes our joy. It is sin, not love. Love is not the villain but the hero. We must love more, not less, and thus, we will suffer more, not less. But we will also have more joy. Christ increases what Buddha removes. If we want to go to Heaven, we must go through Gethsemane and Calvary. Christ's and Buddha's road maps contradict each other.

Buddha's way, the "four noble truths", is strictly logical, but so is Christ's; and Christ's comes to the opposite conclusion: (1) To love on earth is to rehearse for Heaven, for Heaven is Godlikeness, and God is love. (2) But the more you love on earth, the more you will have more sufferings as well as more joy. (3) Therefore, the road to heavenly joy must be through suffering, not away from it.

I confess I am deeply impressed by the genuine peacefulness and kindness of Buddhists. That peacefulness and kindness are so much better than their philosophy, so much more Christlike: if Buddhists are not quite joyful, they are at least enviably cheerful.

But we all need to hope that we are better than our philosophy. God did not promise that any philosophy was the way to Heaven, but He sent us One who claimed, as Buddha never did, "I am the way" (Jn 14:6). Buddha's way is a philosophy; Christ's way is a Person. Buddha claimed to save us by giving us his mind; Christ saved us by giving us His Body. (This means not that Buddhists can't go to Heaven but that their road map is mistaken.)

70

Why Joy *Must* Conquer Sorrow

The whole world is at war. The war began long ago, with Adam's fall—or rather, even earlier, with Satan's—but it seems to be heating up today in our apostate culture. The two sides are not East and West or socialism and capitalism or Democrats and Republicans or Right and Left. Saint Augustine understood the two sides: they are "the city of God" and "the city of the world". Their contrasting philosophies are supernaturalism and naturalism, theistic transcendence and materialistic humanism. John Lennon's song "Imagine" is the imaginary form of this Utopian humanism. Vladimir Lenin's Communism is its nonimaginary form. It has been responsible for more murders than anything else in all of history.

The two sides are not just political but cosmic. Communism, like Nazism, is only one political form of one side of the war, the side on which there is nonbeing, falsehood, evil, ugliness, darkness, death, hate, Hell, and misery. On the other side, there is being, truth, goodness, beauty, light, life, love, Heaven, and joy.

Which side surrounds which? Which outflanks and conquers which? Which has the last word? It is the one that had the first word. The first word is "In the beginning God" (Gen 1:1).

Atheists, nihilists, pessimists, cynics, sophists, materialists, secular humanists, and deconstructionists say that side is fake, false, fantasy, fallacy, foolishness, and fairy tale. That is part of their faith. But reason contradicts this faith. For the dark side is dependent on the light side for its very existence and its essence, or definition. Joy is not the absence of sorrow and misery. If it were, then numbers, rocks, and corpses would have joy. Life is not the absence of death, nor is love merely the absence of hate, nor is peace the mere absence of war. Nonbeing is relative to being, not vice versa, for both its essential meaning (being is not the absence of nonbeing, but vice versa) and its actual occurring (nonbeing and destruction can be caused only by something that has being). Truth defines lies; lies cannot define truth, as cynics and skeptics and deconstructionists claim it can.

The first side is prior also teleologically. The providential purpose for which God allows the second side to exist is for the greater good of the first side. So the first side surrounds the second logically, by definition; metaphysically, in everything real; and teleologically, in terms of purpose. It is also true personally, in terms of love. This is symbolized geometrically by Edwin Markham's poem "Outwitted":

> He drew a circle that shut me out—
> Heretic, a rebel, a thing to flout.
> But Love and I had the wit to win:
> We drew a circle that took him in!

That's why the greatest of poems, Dante's, is the most all-encompassing. And it ends in joy. As Dale Ahlquist, head of the Society of G. K. Chesterton, says,

We read the *Iliad* because all of life is a battle. We read the *Odyssey* because all of life is a journey. We read the Book of Job because all of life is a riddle. We read *Canterbury*

Tales because all of life is a pilgrimage. We read *Don Quixote* because all of life is a knight errantry. We read Shakespeare because all the world's a stage. We read Dickens because all of life is a great expectation. We read Dostoyevsky because we are all part of a family, and every soul is a battleground between heaven and hell. And we read Dante because all of life is a Divine Comedy.[1]

It's all in Augustine. What do they teach them in the schools nowadays, anyway?

---

[1] Quoted in Most Rev. James D. Conley, "Bishop Conley's Address to the Class of 2023: Only the Lover Sings", Thomas Aquinas College, May 20, 2023, https://www.thomasaquinas.edu/news/bishop-conleys-address-class-2023.

71

My Favorite Proof of Original Sin

If joy is thus stronger than misery, why do we feel misery more strongly? Because we all are born with a disease. Three of its names are "selfishness", "stupidity", which is the consequence of selfishness, and "Original Sin", which is the theological explanation for both selfishness and stupidity. "Sin" means literally "separation" (*sünde* in German, *asunder* in Old English)—separation from God. The sins we *do* come from the sinful state in which we *are*.

Original Sin is one of the most radical, and one of the most universally despised, of all Christian dogmas. It means we are not in our right mind, not in our natural human state. We are not normal; we are abnormal. For we are not the norm; we are not the highest being; we are not the most intelligent intelligence. God is.

Yet this radical and despised dogma is provable by experience, simply by reading the newspapers. It explains why we feel death, darkness, evil, and misery more keenly than we feel life, light, goodness, and joy. It is because we are upside down. We are fallen and we can't get up, at least not by ourselves.

Our small sorrows loom larger than our enormous joys. We find resentment easier than gratitude, sin easier than sanctity. That proves not that sin is natural and sanctity unnatural but that we ourselves are unnatural, alienated from our own nature. Our very nature is unnatural! That is also why our feelings are so fallible. We instinctively take them as the standard for judging reality, although reality must be the standard for judging our feelings. (If that were not true, it would be meaningless to try to comfort a two-year-old who dropped his ice cream cone and thought he had just lost the hope of Heaven.) Forgetting that fact is the cause of most of our ridiculous mistakes. Adults are not much more reasonable than two-year-olds, just more sophisticated in their demands and their wars and their weapons.

Only if God exists does this make sense, for then God is the standard of reality, and everything is more real and true and good the more Godlike it is. If God does not exist, then *we* are the highest standard, so our reason judges the (false) idea of God rather than God judging our false idea of ourselves. If God does not exist, we cannot appeal to anything higher than ourselves that is objectively real and not merely subjective and imaginary, nothing that can justify calling ourselves foolish or even wrong. In other words, if God does not exist, we are the infallible court of highest appeal, and our screams at dropping our ice cream cones are valid. (This reductio ad absurdum is an argument for the existence of God. Josiah Royce used it in his chapter entitled "The Possibility of Error" in *The Religious Aspect of Philosophy*.)

The fact that we feel our sorrows more keenly than our joys, and our hates more keenly than our loves, constitutes a strong argument for our fallenness. This must be an illusion, for a privation cannot be stronger than the reality of which it is a privation. Blindness cannot be more than sight, yet we feel it more keenly.

It is the Father of Lies who magnifies our fears and minimizes our joys and makes us think villains are more interesting than heroes in modern stories. Medieval stories were the opposite. That is why we love *The Lord of the Rings* and *The Chronicles of Narnia*. They stand right side up. And therefore we can too.

72

From What Perspective Do We Look at the World?

Here are some of the consequences of the previous point. When we look at this fallen world (i.e., the human world, not the natural world) as the norm, the standard, the center, we see joy as *compensation* for its sorrows, and Heaven as a compensation for earth, as something far off and hardly fit for us, like a palace for a cat. When we see this world as our home, we see Heaven as a vacation or an oasis in our desert.

That is because we are upside down. Heaven is our home, our norm, our center, our standard, our identity. We pray not "Thy kingdom come; Thy will be done in Heaven as it is on earth" but the reverse.

What, then, is this world? It is Heaven's womb. The womb is relative to the world, not vice versa. In fact, the womb is part of the world, and when we look back on this earth from the perspective of Heaven, we will probably see that we were in Heaven (i.e., in Heaven's womb) from the beginning but didn't see that until after death, just as we were in the world already from the moment of our conception but didn't see that until after birth.

That helps to explain why we must suffer: to be made to fit our true home, our authentic identity, which is in

God's mind, not our own. Our true identity is only in His mind, as Hamlet's true identity was in Shakespeare's mind. But God's Mind is the Logos, the eternal preincarnate Christ. Therefore, our very identity is in Christ.

This is God's answer to Job, which was basically, "Your perspective is inside out and upside down. I am not answering your questions because I am not your Answer Man; you are mine. It is I who question you and judge you. You are not My author; I am yours. My name is I AM. I am the "I", and you are the "thou". I am not an ingredient in your religious experience; you are an ingredient in My religious experience."

We seek joy because we were designed for joy and created by divine joy. We lack joy because we are fallen from our original nature and relationship to God. We are not in our natural, rightful condition, and neither is our world. This is a radical idea—as if the whole universe were not in its natural condition.

The fact that joy is extraordinary for us is itself extraordinary. It is abnormal, and a shock, to realize this "abnormalism". It is like discovering that gravity was once subject to our will, or that the speed of light was relative, or that two bodies used to be able to occupy the same space at the same time, until matter "fell".

To our immense relief, God has corrected us and shared His right-side-up perspective with us fallen-down creatures. It's called divine revelation, and its consummation and perfection are not words but *the* Word, Jesus Christ.

73

How Can Sorrows Be Turned into Joys?

Sorrows can become joys by making them into *acts*. Transform your sufferings from receivings into doings, from passivities into activities. That's what Jesus did with the supreme passivity, death (Jn 10:18). "Offer it up" as an act, a gift, a prayer. That doesn't end sufferings, but it transforms them and uses them, which is even better.

Sorrow is passive. It feels as if you're being victimized, smacked down, battered. You feel weak and impotent. You feel falling and failing—failing to get the joy you can't help but desire. Joy, in contrast, is active, like a river. It comes as a surprise and a gift, but you *will* it; you en-joy it, you in-joy it, you swim in its river.

We can turn passive sufferings into acts by offering them to God as oblations, gifts, sacrifices. They are as real as the sacrificial lambs offered in ancient Israel and on the cross. Sufferings are God's gifts to us and our opportunities to make them our gifts to Him. Gifts are freely willed acts, works, deeds, choices, achievements, conquests of the Devil and his temptations to rebellion or despair. Whenever we pray, we *succeed* in praying, no matter how weak the prayer is. There is no such thing as an unsuccessful prayer. When we pray, a new event is inserted into the sum total of reality, and its spiritual gravity makes a difference to the rest of reality.

We can do this even with the supreme suffering of death, as Jesus did with His death, turning this most total passivity into the most total activity, like an author offering his completed book to the publisher.

How do we do that? It is an unanswerable question. We just do it! There is no how, no method, no spiritual technology, no previous cause that determines rather than merely makes possible this effect. This free choice, and every free choice, is a kind of human image of the divine First Cause or Uncaused Cause. It is not a mere link in a causal chain; it creates a new chain. Free choice is creation, not causation. It is, of course, influenced and conditioned, but it is not determined.

How do we make a free choice? Is there a method, a mechanism, a "choice machine" that can grind out choices? No. Then how do we do it? We don't know how we do it, yet we know that we *do* do it. "How" is a question about causality. "How to do x?" means "What y can cause x?" But y cannot be *less* than x because the cause cannot be less than the effect; nothing can give what it does not have. But there is nothing greater that we can do than the free choices called faith, hope, love, and prayer. No buttons or keys for them.

Joy is the effect of faith, hope, and love. It is one of the fruits of the Holy Spirit, not of the human spirit alone. Nothing in us alone can be the adequate cause of this joy or of the faith, hope, and love from which it flows—no method for "doing" them, no spiritual technology—because joy is personal, and persons, unlike machines, have free will. Prayers, works, joys, and sufferings; faith, hope, and love; adoration, thanksgiving, reparation, and petition are all personal acts of both ourselves and God in co-operation.

There are really four persons in this, for the whole Trinity is acting in everything God does. Deterministic materialism says there are no free and responsible persons there (or anywhere else). Atheistic humanism says there is only one. Judaism and Islam say there are two. Christianity says there are four.

74

City of Joy

If you have never read the excellent book *The City of Joy* or seen the movie that is its travesty, you will never guess what city it refers to. It's Calcutta, the world's most famous slum, at least before its moderate improvements in the twenty-first century. It's Mother Teresa's Calcutta, though she is not in the book or the movie.

The book, by the famous French journalist Dominique Lapierre, coauthor of *Is Paris Burning?*, tells the true story of three men who go to Calcutta: a Catholic priest in spiritual crisis, a starving Hindu farmer from the country, and an unbelieving Jewish doctor from Miami with a social conscience. But the real protagonist of the book is Calcutta itself, especially its leper colony.

The title *The City of Joy* is *not* ironic. The author was amazed to find deep and genuine joy in that horribly poor place. One can romanticize moderate poverty, as does Thoreau, but one cannot romanticize Calcutta. Think of living under cardboard on the street. No running water. Scrounging in garbage dumps for food and for tiny sellable throwaway items. Having to bribe officials for nearly all public services. Restaurants whose choicest item is advertised as "meat". No plumbing. Sharing beds with fleas, roaches, and rats. Now add to that leprosy. Where could the "joy" possibly come from? It is real, so it has to come from somewhere.

The answer is true not just for Calcutta but also for the rest of the world. The joy comes from the one sure source it always comes from. There are many words for it: *agape*, charity, love, friendship, unselfishness, giving, generosity, sharing, community, mercy, compassion, unselfishness.

To live in Calcutta and be in love is a joy. To live in Hawaii and not be in love is not a joy. Suffering shared can be a joy; pleasure kept to oneself cannot.

The poorer you are, the more you give away. Those who can least afford to be generous are the most generous. Those who can afford the largest proportion of their stuff give the smallest. Also, the richer you are, the less you depend on your family. The poorer you are, the more you rely on your family and the more your society is an extended family. Impersonal economic systems are our inventions; families are God's. They work. No merely human invention ever gave more joy than family. (And, because *corruptio optimi pessima*, it also produces more sorrow. "Lilies that fester smell far worse than weeds."[1])

The Church is a large extended family, God's family, God's kids. Augustine called it "the City [*civitas*, community, common unity] of God". The Church is an institution and a hierarchy and an authority, but first of all, it is a family. It is not "the business of God" but "the People of God". It magnifies and multiplies our joy (see Saint Anselm on this, pensées 24 and 60).

The City of Joy is empirical evidence that Romans 8:28 is true not just in Heaven, in hope, but also on earth, in experience. The poor smile the most, give the most, live the most, love the most, and enjoy the little that they have the most. They use the words "blessing" and "blessed" for little things; the rich do not use those words even for

---

[1] William Shakespeare, "Sonnet 94", line 14.

big things. If you doubt this, ask Dorothy Day's Catholic Worker people or the Knights of Malta or Mother Teresa's Missionaries of Charity, who deal with real people, not just statistics, agencies, experts, politics, and ideologies. They often say, "I'm blessed"—and they are. The rich usually don't—and aren't.

75

The Stupidest Prize in the World

Each year, the "experts" at the World Happiness Project pick out what they consider the five happiest nations and the five unhappiest nations in the world. Nearly every year, the happiest nations are the five Scandinavian nations, and the unhappiest are in sub-Saharan Africa.

When I first discovered this, I thought it was a great joke, a prank. For the clearest and most universal manifestation of happiness is a smile—even preliterate infants understand that—and the clearest proof of unhappiness is suicide. And no subcontinent smiles more and commits suicide less than sub-Saharan Africa, and no subcontinent smiles less and commits suicide more than Scandinavia. So it's a joke, right? Everyone remarks about those dour, unsmiling Africans and those "don't worry, be happy", devil-may-care, smiling, dancing Scandinavians, right?

Africa has grinding poverty, disease, corrupt political regimes, violent terrorists, and fewer freedoms and powers than the rest of the world, while Scandinavia has the most comfortable incomes, universal health care, beautiful scenery, short workweeks, higher pay, "progressive" social systems, more freedoms, "alternative lifestyles", safe "sex workers", and readily available contraception, abortion, and euthanasia. Yet Africans have the most smiles and the fewest suicides. How do the "experts" explain that data?

Perhaps they think that the smiles are fake. Perhaps they think that the suicides are fake too. Perhaps only dollars are data.

Perhaps the "experts" at the World Happiness Project have never heard of smiles. Perhaps they never saw them. After all, how could the poor possibly be happy, or "blessed", as was said by that primitive, naïve Rabbi whose name has been forgotten or banished from all polite and political conversation in places like Scandinavia but is alive and growing in places like Africa?

I think I know why the "experts" judged as they did. They are slaves to technology, to science and mathematics, and to the digital data a computer can digest. You can measure exactly how much money you have but not how much joy or despair you have. To those who live in the Matrix, only what fits into a computer's data banks is real, and that means quantification. It is the ideal of any science to be "exact"—i.e., quantified. To the merely mathematical-mechanical mind, quality is only a confused, subjective, and prescientific version of quantity.

That idea is so ridiculous that only a Ph.D. could believe it. There are some ideas that can be believed only by "experts" with "advanced degrees"—advanced degrees of insanity. Some "experts" need not refutations but psychiatrists—or exorcists.

76

The Two Halves of Life

Life presents us all, in all times, places, cultures, religions, ideologies, genders, ages, temperaments, and levels of education, with two things: there is Good News and there is Bad News.

There is good and there is evil. There is life and there is death. There is sanctity and there is sin. There is peace and there is war. There is truth and there is falsehood. There is knowledge and there is ignorance. There is beauty and there is ugliness. There is Heaven and there is Hell. There is salvation and there is damnation. There is hate and there is love. (There is also neither, which is "I don't give a damn", which is damnation.) There is being and there is nonbeing. There are stars and there are black holes. There is light and there is darkness. There is pleasure and there is pain. There is happiness and there is unhappiness. There is joy and there is misery.

There is rest and there is restlessness. Restlessness is good, even though it is not joyful, because it seeks a great good—namely, true joy; and all who honestly seek eventually find. If you wonder why it often takes so long, read Augustine's *Confessions*.

The saints don't deny either of life's two halves. Sinners deny deep joy, but saints don't deny deep misery.

Unbelievers deny Heaven, but believers don't deny Hell. Which of the two is simplistic?

Jean-Jacques Rousseau taught that we are born good and that evil comes from outside, from our society. Thomas Hobbes taught that we are born evil and selfish and that good comes from outside, from social force and fear. Marx taught that we are neither good nor evil but malleable, like clay, shaped but not shapers, matter but not spirit. Common sense and Christianity teach that we are by nature both good and evil and that, as Solzhenitsyn famously said, the line between good and evil runs through the middle of every human heart.[1]

And since joy comes from good and not evil, life is a spiritual war between good and evil and therefore between joy and misery. To deny either of these enormous halves of life is an inexcusable oversimplification. Yet these two oversimplifications are both more common than common sense.

[1] Aleksandr Solzhenitsyn, *The Gulag Archipelago: An Experiment in Literary Investigation*, vol. 2, repr. ed. (New York: HarperCollins, 2007).

77

The Secret of the Joy of the Saints

Where can we see joy? In my eighty-seven years, I've met and talked with thousands of people, privately and publicly, in each of the fifty states and thirteen countries, and I have never, ever met any who were more deeply and radiantly full of joy than Mother Teresa's Missionaries of Charity. It's no contest. A slam dunk. (They're not the only ones. The Carmelite contemplative nuns are up there too.) So what's their secret?

It's the most unsecret secret in history. It's not an "it" but a "who". It's the most famous person in history. It's Jesus Himself, the God who is love incarnated in human form. The Missionaries of Charity are literally the missionaries of *that* charity. That's the secret of their joy.

They get up early in the morning and spend two or three hours in prayer and adoration in front of the Blessed Sacrament. Why? Because that's where Jesus is really, truly, literally, fully present. They spend lots of time there simply because the two things they love the most are to love Him and be loved by Him. Love always wants to get closer.

They eat plainly and sparingly. They own only two sets of clothes. Their only possessions are cleaning tools. They spend their days looking for the most broken people, broken families, broken lives, and broken hearts, and they help them pick up the pieces, both materially and spiritually.

They seek out Calcuttas in the South Bronx and Rox-
bury and Detroit. They do what Jesus did. And their joy is
unmistakable and unfakeable.

Most of their members in America come not from
America but from India or Mexico. When I asked them
why, the answer was that most American girls fear such
radical, terrible, wonderful, quiet, radiant joy. They prefer
their little *manageable* joys and sorrows, their creature comforts, the things we *can't* take with us when we die, instead
of the one thing we *can*: the presence of Jesus and His joy
in the soul that has been given to Him.

That particular vocation, to that particular order, of
course, is not for everyone. The Catholic Church is very
fat, i.e., large, i.e., catholic, i.e., universal. There are many
other ways of living the joy of Jesus' presence externally.
But there is no other way internally, because there is no
other Person who can give it to us, for the simple reason
that Jesus alone is God. Socrates, Buddha, Muhammad,
Moses, Lao Tzu, Confucius, and Elvis are not God. Their
joy and peace are not the joy and peace that the world cannot give (Jn 14:27). Jesus' joy is. It's supernatural because
He is supernatural.

It's almost an equation. It's scandalously simple. It's all
one thing, a seamless web: God, His Christ, His will, His
love, His joy.

I will tell you about the one time in my life I know I
was inspired by the Holy Spirit, because I'm smart enough
to know that I'm not smart enough to come up with the
answer I gave all by myself. I had just given a talk to some
monks in Connecticut, and at the end of the Q and A ses-
sion, just before I left, the abbot said to me, "We always ask
our visitors this last question: If God promised you that He
would give us any gift you asked Him for, what gift would
you ask Him to give us?" The question was so unexpected

that I had no time to think of anything clever or original, so I just said, "That every one of you would fall totally in love with Jesus Christ for every moment of your life." The monks began to laugh, and the abbot explained, "We're laughing because Mother Teresa was here last month, and that's exactly the answer she gave us."

78

Seven Obstacles to Joy

What are some obstacles to joy?

The first is unbelief. If you don't believe that the God who is love exists, you can't love Him or be loved by Him. And that's where joy comes only from. Orange juice comes only from oranges. To find pearls, get oysters.

The second is unrepented sin, which makes you God's enemy (though He is never your enemy), the cop you run from rather than the Father you run to.

The third is self-centeredness, which refuses to take its eyes off itself—its own troubles, fears, and inadequacies— and look to the cause of all joy. Ingrown eyeballs are as joyless as ingrown toenails.

The fourth is fear: fear of the sacrifices and sufferings that sanctity demands, coupled with doubt that suffering out of love can actually increase your joy. Satan inserts these fears and lies into your feelings.

The fifth is boredom, acedia, spiritual sloth, having a dishrag heart and a spaghetti spine, refusing to get up out of bed. The bed is yourself.

The sixth is a kind of spiritual attention deficit disorder, refusing to tame and train and focus your attention on God. Another profound truth that Buddha knew was the truth in the first sentence of the most popular of all Buddhist scriptures, the Dhammapada: "All that we are depends on what we have thought." The dependence of the will on the mind is just as real as the dependence of the mind on the will. To move, you need both the fuel of the will and the road map of the mind.

The seventh is greedy and lustful desires. They were Buddha's primary enemies. He knew that they tear you apart because they divide you into what you want versus what you have. They tear you apart by sending you to many idols, false gods, and false hopes. Buddha didn't know the true God, but he knew these false gods very clearly, as Jesus did.

Søren Kierkegaard wrote that "purity of heart is to will one thing."[1] Desiring, loving, and willing many things makes you into many things. It tears your peace into pieces, for you are whatever you love. Your desires, like animals in a zoo, are all hungry and demanding, and they cannot all be satisfied. This joyless philosophy of life, seeing yourself as the zookeeper, is seen most clearly in the demoniac who confesses, "My name is Legion; for we are many" (Mk 5:9).

[1] Søren Kierkegaard, *Purity of Heart Is to Will One Thing* (n.p.: Rough Draft Publishing, 2013), 85.

79

The Argument One More Time

An *argument* for joy? Isn't that bizarre? Not at all. Reason
and argument can keep you sane. They can also keep you
in the faith. The problem is this: If God loves us, why do
we have such misery?

We have only five options logically.

The first option is to believe that we are wrong and God
is right about whether our sufferings are necessary for our
greatest good. We have no clear idea about whether they
are necessary for our greatest good because we are only
characters in His play; He is not a character in ours. But we
do have one very clear idea about who we are: we are not
God, and therefore we are in no position either to prove
or to disprove the "faith hypothesis". So we must either
believe it or believe one of its four possible alternatives.

The second option is to believe that there simply is no
God; that all the wise and holy saints, sages, mystics, and
prophets and billions of honest, sane, simple believers—
and, above all, Jesus Himself—were deluded by the greatest hoax in history; that wisdom on this most weighty and
life-changing issue of all can be found in only the few, the
arrogant, the atheists, almost all of whom are clustered in
one culture in one small time and place—namely, modern
Western post-Christian culture; and, therefore, that the vast
majority of mankind has always been doing what Jimmy

Stewart did in the old movie *Harvey*—namely, believing in a large, invisible, imaginary rabbit as his best friend and the center of his life. Freud was honest enough to call this (i.e., religious faith, belief in a super-Harvey) literally insanity. That doesn't disprove atheism; it just classifies it: snobbery.

The third option is to believe that God is stupid—in fact, stupider than we are, for He fails to see how bad our sufferings are, as we do; that's why He does not do what is easy for Him to do—namely, just take them away.

The fourth option is to believe that God is weaker than drugs or doctors are, that He *cannot* take away our sufferings, as drugs and doctors can. All He can do is look on them with pity and weep with us, as a spectator, not an actor.

The fifth option is to believe that we suffer because God does not love us and does not want to deliver us, that He is a cosmic sadist who loves to see us suffer—in fact, that He and Satan are the same being. Or perhaps God just doesn't give a damn about us, which is, in a way, even worse, for to be hated is at least to be noticed and cared about, if only as an enemy.

Make your choice, then. Make a Pascal's wager. Which alternative is the least unreasonable one? And which one offers us the possibility of joy in the end?

Each requires faith, but I don't have enough faith to choose the other four. That's my "argument".

80

God's Love as the Cause
of Our Deepest Joy

When Saint Philip Neri was in his twenties, God showed him how overwhelmingly great His love for him was. Fittingly, the overwhelming divine love overwhelmed Philip. Its joy was so unendurable that he rolled on the floor and prayed and pleaded with God to stop!

If you are a romantic lover, a little smile of love on a pretty woman's face has the power to cause the delightfully discombobulating joy of butterflies in your stomach. How much more joy-making power is there in the infinite love of the infinitely beautiful God that was manifested on the cross for you, despite all your faults, fears, fallacies, and fantasies, all your worries, warts, and wickedness? And how much more joy-making power will there be in the face-to-face of the Beatific Vision? For God is not only infinite truth and infinite goodness but also infinite beauty.

We do not usually *feel* this joy in our emotions, as Saint Philip did for a short time. If we did, it would be unendurable and we would have to pray what he prayed. But we *know* it is true; we know that the infinite divine love that has the power to cause our eternal and unlimited joy is really there because God, who can neither deceive nor be deceived, has infallibly revealed it—in Christ, in the teachings of the Church He founded and authorized to teach in

His name, in her divinely inspired Scriptures, and in her saints. No matter how subjectively uncertain we may feel, nothing is more objectively certain than that.

As earth's atmosphere and clouds temper the sun's light and heat, our souls' emotional atmosphere and clouds do the same to the Son's rays of truth and love. God temporarily removed the clouds for Saint Philip.

Faith is an X-ray vision through the clouds. It is not a feeling or an opinion or even merely a belief (although it is also a belief); it is a knowing. It may not be proved, it may be doubted, but it is knowledge—knowledge of reality. It is the knowledge of a love that is unlimited, unconditional, unqualified, unending, infinite, infallible, incomprehensible, invulnerable, nonjudgmental, and nonnegotiable. It is not impersonal and general and abstract; it is personal and individual and concrete. It is more like romance than philanthropy.

God is totally "single-minded". He is love. Period. Love is not just one of His attributes. It is His essence. It is His love itself that *has* all the other attributes, including power and wisdom. It is love that is all-wise and all-powerful. It is all-conquering by its own lovely essence.

The next time something horrible happens to you, ask yourself, Do I believe that God is deliberately allowing this only because He loves me more than I can know? If you believe that, tell Him. And tell Him also if you don't, and then ask Him for the faith that is His gift. After all, where do you think your faith, hope, and love came from? He is the First Cause of everything good. There are not many first causes of goodness and thus, ultimately, of joy; there is only one.

The eyes of Christ in an icon are not meant to be examined as objects of art or science, for they are looking at you, not you at them. The cross is the ultimate icon. The next time you doubt Christ's love, just look at a crucifix.

81

God's Power as a Cause of Our Joy

I remember a haunting line from a movie I saw long ago. A young, idealistic, charismatic, and handsome priest in a corrupt Latin American country has been fighting year after year against poverty and misery among his parishioners and against corruption and oppression in both church and state, both of which see him as a threat and plot to have him killed. He is also fighting against ongoing temptations from a beautiful woman who is in love with him. One day, the straw breaks the camel's back, and he simply gives up. The priest and the beautiful woman leave the town and live together in a little hut in the jungle. Just as the viewer suspects the movie of siding with the sexual revolution, it turns. Their relationship becomes strained and silent. One night, the woman wakes up to find the priest gone. Her face and body language show that she expected this and knows what to do. She follows the road to a little chapel, and there he is, alone, prone on the floor, weeping before the Eucharist. She says, "I knew it would come to this. You're going back, aren't you?"

"Yes", he says.

"I don't understand. I know you love me, and you know they hate you and you are probably going to be martyred. Just tell me why you're going back to them and not to me."

He points to the exposed Host on the altar and blurts out, "He ... is ... stronger."

God's strength is not control or force. Yet it is divine and therefore omnipotent. It manifests itself, paradoxically, not first of all in a crown of gold but in a crown of thorns. That crown looks like weakness and failure; it is, in fact, the strongest power in the universe: suffering love. Those two things work together like an epoxy glue. The Devil did not understand that; if he did, he would not have inspired his agents Judas, Pilate, Caiaphas, and the Romans to arrange Christ's Crucifixion, which was apparently the worst thing that ever happened but which was really our *Good* Friday, our salvation, and the Devil's definitive defeat.

Love without suffering is good but not strong. Suffering without love is strong but not good. Modern Western Christians prefer love without suffering, Christ without the cross; Islamic terrorists embrace martyrdom but without Christ and His love. Neither the crossless Christ nor the Christ-less cross will win the world.

Nehemiah 8:10 says that "the joy of the LORD is your strength." The Nazis perverted this truth in naming their training program "Strength through Joy". Their joy was in force, not in freedom; in hate, not in love. We see what that false "strength" and "joy" come to in the end most clearly in Hitler's suicide.

82

The First Supernatural
Bank and Trust Company

The connection between faith and joy is trust. Trust comes from faith (you trust only someone you have faith in) and leads to joy (the trust in the eyes of the baby looking up at his mother's face is what puts the smile of joy on his face). Trust is essentially a form of hope, which is faith directed toward the future. It entrusts the future to God. He is our First Supernatural Bank and Trust Company. (To "bank" on someone is to trust him.)

The intellectual dimension of faith is an act of the intellect, prompted by the will, by which we believe all that has been revealed by God, who can neither deceive nor be deceived. Faith also has a "heart" dimension, in two senses of "heart": (1) the spiritual emotions, such as trust, and (2) the nonobjectifiable, indefinable center of the self, the "I" we mean when we speak of "my" soul, "my" intellect, "my" choices, and "my" body. It is the "pre-functional root" (philosopher Herman Dooyeweerd's term) of all the soul's functions. Solomon pointed to this when he wrote, "Keep thy heart with all diligence; for out of it are the issues of life" (Prov 4:23, KJV).

When we offer God all our prayers, works, joys, and sufferings in the Morning Offering, it is easy to understand

three of the four. Whom should we pray to and worship
and adore but God? For whom should we work and live
but God? And who alone can transform and redeem our
sufferings but God? But what do we do when we offer
Him our joys?

We give Him *authority* over them. We give Him per-
mission to take them away if He wills, because we trust
Him who loves us so much that He gave His Son's life
for us: "For our sake he [the Father] made him [Christ] to
be sin who knew no sin, so that in him we might become
the righteousness of God" (2 Cor 5:21). It was the Great
Exchange: Christ entered our Hell ("My God, my God,
why have you forsaken me?" [Mt 27:46]) so that we could
enter His Heaven.

That is why we trust Him even with our most precious
joys. We "invest" them in His First Supernatural Bank
and Trust Company, like a farmer "investing" seeds in the
earth so that many more will sprout. They pay compound
interest in the resurrection. The God of life will resurrect
not only our dead bodies but also our dead joys. That is
why we bury our dead in the earth: because the earth is a
holy sign, a God-designed icon of resurrection. Because
we trust Him, we invest our joy-seeds in His loving will,
which is like investing seeds in the life-giving earth.

83

Simplicity as a Cause of Our Joy

I think the very simplest prayer that brings us joy is the five words of Saint Faustina's "Jesus, I trust in You."

It is the prayer of a child. We have it on the highest authority that "unless you turn and become like children, you will never enter the kingdom of heaven" (Mt 18:3).

Christ didn't say "remain" as children but "turn and become" like children. It's the mature, free, rational, discriminating adult who must become like a child. We are to become adult children instead of childish adults.

Simplicity *works*. What Confucius said was almost always simple and obvious, even boring. But he invented the most successful social philosophy in history, holding together the world's largest nation for the longest time in relative peace, prosperity, and happiness.

Aristotle's philosophy is simple and obvious too, and commonsensical, beneath its technical terminology. That's why it's ignored or despised by nearly every "great" original philosopher after Aquinas.

Your soul is simple, though it has many powers. It cannot be cut into pieces, as you yourself can (body versus soul) and as your body can (limbs, organs, cells, molecules, atoms, subatomic particles).

Monogamy is simpler than polygamy—and more joyful.

God is the simplest of all realities. No divisions, no parts, no conflicts. When our relation to Him becomes simpler, we ourselves become simpler, more Godlike, and more joyful.

A simple kiss or an "I love you" gives us more joy than a complete, complex psychoanalysis. How much anguish, confusion, frustration, and waste would be overcome simply by simplicity? Like Lao Tzu's "knowing that enough is enough, is enough" (*Tao Te Ching*). Like God's capping all His words (in the plural) with *the* Word (in the singular).

So go there. Start with simplicity. Don't just read it and think it. Say it and mean it, now: "Jesus, I trust in You!" And then observe the difference that makes. Observe what happens to your facial muscles.

84

Hope and a Joyful Death

Philosopher Gabriel Marcel sees death as the test of hope. And hope is obviously a cause of joy. But death seems to give the lie to hope. In death, we seem to lose everything and gain nothing. We seem to lose our very being, our whole being, and thus all our joy.

One answer to that doubt about life after death is very simple for anyone but an atheist. It is that even if we did lose our whole being in death, God could restore our being again and re-create it from nothingness just as He created it in our beginning from nothingness. For God alone can create in the proper sense of that word. Creation is not simply making, shaping a preexisting material into a new form. Creation makes something out of nothing, creates the whole being, matter and form together. Even if the soul died with the body, God could create not just a new, identical twin soul (which would be not you but your twin) but the same soul—your unique individual soul—again, since God is not in time or bound by time.

Hope allows a "happy death", even a joyful death—death as a conquest, death as a gift, death as a mercy, though "a severe mercy" (Sheldon Vanauken's great title). Satan invented death as a curse, but God transformed it into a gift. It would be terrible if God had not given us the gift of death or if we could circumvent it, either by creeping

past the cherubim's flaming sword that prevented Adam
and Eve from going back into Eden to eat the fruit of the
other tree, the tree of (eternal) life, or by our scientists'
discovering the cure for death itself by genetic engineer-
ing (which many of them believe is possible and some are
actually working on). If we did not have the gift of death,
we would have Hell on earth. As C. S. Lewis said, "We
are like eggs at present. And you cannot go on indefinitely
being just an ordinary, decent egg. We must be hatched
or go bad."[1] If you want to see (or, rather, smell) what our
world would be like if our genetic engineers succeeded in
inventing artificial immortality, just leave a dozen eggs on
your kitchen table for a year.

Hope allows us a happy death by allowing us to trust
God to conquer death, as Christ did with Lazarus, with
Jairus' daughter, and with the son of the widow at Nain
and as His Father did with Him. More than that, though,
we need not just a second chance but a second nature, one
that could endure eternity without rotting, without sin.
Our hope is not just for immortality but also for sanctity—
that after death we who are in Christ by faith and Baptism will never again experience the worst thing there is,
which is not pain or death but sin. Saint Alphonsus Liguori
thought that freedom from all sin was the greatest joy in
death (*Preparation for Death*, consideration 5).

Even more than that negative thing, that absence of sin,
God promises us the positive new life that is a share in His
own divine life (*zoe*) and joy forever, in the "new birth".

This sharing in divine life is literally unimaginable.
Divine revelation defines the joys of Heaven in the only
way we can understand—namely, as something we cannot
understand: "No eye has seen, nor ear heard, nor the heart

---

[1] C. S. Lewis, *Mere Christianity* (New York: HarperOne, 1952), 199.

of man conceived, what God has prepared for those who love him" (1 Cor 2:9). All our positive conceptions of God and Heaven are as radically inadequate as a dog's understanding of human things or an infant's understanding of adult things. All the mystics in all religions who have had some foretaste of this heavenly life agree on one thing: it cannot be put into words. It is "unutterable and exalted joy" (1 Pet 1:8).

85

Charity as a Cause of Our Joy

There is no joy without charity (*agape*, self-giving love). Joy is the fulfillment of the self, and this comes only by what is apparently its opposite: the loss of self, voluntarily giving yourself away to others. Every religion in the world knows some aspect of this mystery. Even Buddhism, which believes in no soul, self, God, or life after death, insists on the radical death of egotism.

But the *joy* of charity is often blocked even when charity itself is present. It is blocked not only by selfishness and sin but also by fear, worry, and feelings of despair even when the freely chosen active intentions and deeds of charity are present. I know this from personal experience, and I suspect you do too.

The only cure for these faults (and they are faults) is faith and hope in God's grace to remove them and, when God does *not* remove them, the faith that His not-doings, as well as all His doings, are done for the one motive that drives everything He does in our lives: His love for us and our greatest good and greatest joy in the end. God is really very, very simple-hearted.

The cure is not just to believe this but to confess to God in prayer that we believe it: to confess both our faults and our faith. Our faith need not be perfect (is it ever?) for us to confess this honestly: "I believe; help my unbelief!" (Mk 9:24).

Fear impedes joy. So what takes away fear? Love. "Perfect love casts out fear" (1 Jn 4:18). Love and fear are like fire and water. For fear is self-referential, self-conscious, self-doubting, while love is self-forgetful, conscious only of God's will and the neighbor's needs.

But it takes a lifetime or more to grow perfect love. We are like plants, not machines. We grow slowly, not instantly. So what can we do right now?

We can begin.

86

The Communion of Saints
as a Cause of Our Joy

A most powerful cause of joy is the presence and communion of others whom we love and who love us. For joy never comes to the self from the self alone but always from others. How could the self give to itself a joy it does not have?

The communion of saints (in Heaven, on earth, and *between* the two places) is one of the twelve articles of the earliest and most basic creed, the Apostles' Creed. And communion, or community, or friendship, is a cause of great joy. *All* the saved and sanctified are saints in the most basic, biblical sense. Saints are simply one kind of sinners, since sin is what all of us have in common. ("All have sinned and fall short of the glory of God" [Rom 3:23].) The Church names a few thousand of them, assures us that they are in Heaven, offers them to us for our imitation and inspiration, and counsels us to pray to them for their prayers to God for us. We are humbly to petition our petitioners. And humility is also a cause of great joy, after the first shock.

It is reasonable to believe that these perfected saints in Heaven know, love, help, and pray for us saints-in-training on earth because if *you* were in Heaven and someone you knew and loved were still on earth, your love would move you to pray for him. Your love will surely not shrink in Heaven! And the perfected saints whom the Church names for us have more powerful love, more heavenly "influence" than we have. Asking others to pray for us is a realistic and practical act of humility, whether those others are on earth or in Heaven.

It is not accidental if you were named after a saint. Orthodox Jews pray to God before naming a baby, asking God to guide their choice, because a name is not merely a convenient human label but part of divine providence and part of our identity. Nor is it accidental that your personality and life experiences often lead you to identify with, or find a key to your identity in, a particular saint. It is providential and not accidental if you have found a concrete example of your divinely predestined identity as a saint in Justin or Augustine, in Francis or Thomas, in Theresa or Kateri, in Monica or Mary. It is a joy to discover your identity.

There is no communion of saints in Hell, because there are no saints and because there is no communion. There is terrible aloneness, without communion, community, friendship, charity, or "witness". Heaven is the total opposite of Hell in this, as in all other ways, for Heaven has the most intimate and most powerful withness, or communion. This communion is "a great multitude which no man could number" (Rev 7:9) of friends who are not only human but also angelic and divine (the Three who are one God). They will help make our death itself as *easy* as the process of dying is hard, for we will be in the hands of others, especially God's angelic instruments, who will "carry" our souls to God. Most powerful of all is God's mother, to whom we ask in every Hail Mary to "pray for us ... now and at the hour of our death", the two most important moments in our lives.

In Heaven, we will never again be alone or want to be alone. On earth, it is often good to be alone and to want to be alone for a while. Even Jesus withdrew often from the human crowds for solitary communion with His Father. It is eerily significant that our society deems solitude not a gift or a privilege, as Jesus and the saints saw it, but as our cruelest imaginable punishment, which we impose on our worst criminals!

Two sentences we will never say or hear in Heaven are "Too many people here!" and "Leave me alone!"

87

Mary as "Cause of Our Joy"

There is a beautiful scene in *The Passion of the Christ* in which Mary, on the Via Dolorosa, agonizes over her inability to help Jesus physically as He carries His cross (and our sins). We see in her mind a flashback of Jesus as a little boy falling, hurting Himself, crying, and coming to His mother for comfort; and she, of course, kisses His boo-boo and compassionately comforts Him. She can no longer do that for Him at His Passion. That is her greatest agony.

She can, however, still be with Him in His pain—and even in His death! Look at the *Pietà*—there He is in her arms again! She is uniting her pain with His, becoming our co-redeemer, His co-operator. She is not passive, and neither are we. We do, less perfectly, what she did, both we and she in total dependence on Him.

God designed motherhood. He didn't have to; angels have no mothers. Mothers are (and do) something fathers cannot be (or do); if that were not so, God would not have created two sexes. The perverting or undoing of this unique "image of God" that Scripture identifies as "male and female" (Gen 1:27) is the most destructive heresy of our time. It is Satan's attack on the archetypal essence of both motherhood and fatherhood, reducing both to biological accidents, not designed or meaningful or spiritually significant. This cuts the human person in two (as does death, into a soulless body and a bodiless soul). It makes the person into an angel trapped in the body of an animal; a subjective spirit chained to an objective body; a ghost in a haunted house, which it tries to claim, own, manipulate, redesign, and re-create according to its own mind and will. It says "My will be done" instead of "Thy will be done" over the most precious body in the universe: the human body.

Satan cannot harm God, but he can horribly harm the image of God in man. At this time, our "progressive" media are massively and enthusiastically doing Satan's work. My local newspaper, the *Boston Globe*, has turned into a 100 percent uniform, politically correct propaganda sheet for the entire sexual revolution and especially for transgenderism. What used to be a newspaper has become a missionary enterprise, an evangelistic campaign for the new religion of Man as God. Adolf Hitler has proved to be a prophet: as he predicted, "the Big Lie" has proved to be easier to convince the public of than little lies.

Our two strongest spiritual allies in fighting this attack on the image of God are Mary and Joseph. One of the titles the Litany of Loreto gives to Mary is "cause of our joy", for Jesus is our joy, and Mary gives us Jesus. She did that spiritually when she said Yes to the angel of the Annunciation; and she did it materially in the Nativity; and she keeps doing it supernaturally by her intercession with the King, as Queen of Heaven. She still mothers her children. Look what she did at Lepanto, at Guadalupe, and at Fátima. The Devil fears this mighty warrior more than he fears all the angels in Heaven. And she is always smiling a Mona Lisa smile of deepest joy. She acts especially in times of great sin, sorrow, and suffering, like our time.

Don't stop praying her Rosary. No matter how bad you are at praying, the Rosary is easy. It was Pope Saint John Paul II's favorite prayer. It's not just an exercise to make you more pious; it's a weapon to save the world from Hell. It is Mary's heavenly joy to answer our prayers. She is still a mother, and a mother after God's own heart, which is never cold. A "cold-hearted mother" is almost as self-contradictory as a "joyless God". God is called "He" rather than "She" in all Jewish, Christian, and Muslim scriptures, not because He lacks any of the perfections of the women who constitute half of "the image of God" but because He impregnates us, not we Him. Our joy is to receive Him as Mary received the Holy Spirit, her divine Spouse, to become pregnant with divine life. Luke 1:35 is addressed to us as well as to Mary. Like Jesus, she is for us the rule, not the exception.

88

Angels as a Cause of Our Joy

We are never alone but always in a crowd that we do not see. We are surrounded not only by billions of human beings—both the saints in Heaven, whom we do not see, and those still in basic training on earth, whom we do see—but also by even more persons without bodies, beings who are vastly superior to us in both quantity and quality of mind and will: angels. Since each individual has his own guardian angel, and since the guardian angels are on the lowest rung of the angelic hierarchy, there must be far more angels than humans. And just as the presence, attention, love, and care of humans give us joy, so do those of the angels.

The reality of angels is a dogma, a definitive divine revelation. They appear surrounding almost every important event in the Bible. If angels are only myths, then the whole fabric of the biblical story is a myth. Every religion in the world believes in something like angels: superhuman finite creatures, the true extraterrestrials. They fill the cosmic gap between us and God as animals fill the gap between us and plants.

They are *Jesus'* angels. They are relative to Him, not He to them. They sing. They shine. They praise. They fight. They conquer. They are glorious. These are only six of the many reasons they give us joy.

We do not see them because they are not part of the material universe. They do not have bodies, though they can "assume" bodies as disguises. The good ones do God's will perfectly and therefore do only good, not evil, whether they light or lead, guide or guard, comfort or warn. Many of them are God's "messengers", God's "media" to us. Others simply contemplate God in tireless joy and glory in Heaven.

There are also evil angels, fallen angels, demons, who are our enemies, unless the Church, Scripture, and Jesus Himself lie to us. We "contend" with them (Eph 6:12). As the good angels share with us their joy, the fallen angels share with us their misery. If we saw these creatures as they are, we would fall on our faces in terror for the fallen angels and in thanksgiving for the good angels, who are stronger and who protect us from them. Thus, life is a joy, but life is also a battle.

All our angel art limps, yet it always suggests the same thing: joy, praise, glory, light. When we see the real angels, we will be embarrassed at how much we underestimated them even in our best art. Tolkien (in *The Silmarillion*) and C. S. Lewis (in his Space Trilogy) give me the most credible verbal art about them that I know.

Joy is one of the things the good angels give us, humbly and anonymously. The last time you suddenly felt joy without any apparent cause, that was probably an angel doing his usual work. The same is true of good ideas. We often don't know where they come from. I'm often asked where I get the ideas for so many books (more than one hundred so far). I honestly have no idea, but I know it's not just from me. I strongly suspect it's mainly from the angels.

Pray often to the Lord of angels to send His angels into your mind and your spiritual emotions to fight for you against your enemies. They are His angels, after all, and He delegates them and their work in our behalf above all to Mary, His mother, who is the "Queen of Angels".

When you pray for joy, pray for angels.

89

Beauty as a Cause of Our Joy

We experience joy whenever we see beauty. Saint Thomas defines beauty very simply as "that which, when seen, pleases" (*id quod visum placet*). He says that "although the beautiful and the good are identical in the subject (the real things of which they are properties), they are different in concept (definition). For the good, which is what all desire, properly has to do with the idea of an end (goal, value, purpose), while beauty has to do with knowledge (intellection, understanding, contemplation), for we call those things beautiful which please us when they are seen (whether seen with the senses or the mind)."[1]

The ancient Greeks knew the identity of beauty and goodness better than we do. They gave their greatest poets free room and board in the town hall for life; we expect ours to scrounge or starve, or at least to be social rebels.

The practical point is that beauty is not practical. It is contemplative. Just *seeing* beauty, even the little natural beauties we see here every day, is joy because it is a tiny foretaste of the supernatural beauty we will see in the Beatific Vision, which is our supreme joy. Just seeing it. You can't *do* anything with beauty: use it, buy it, sell it, conquer it. You just look at it, and it gives you joy as the sun gives you light.

[1] *ST* I, q. 5, art. 4, ad 1.

Saint Thomas listed three essential properties of beauty: integrity (i.e., perfection, lacking nothing), harmony (proportion), and clarity (brightness and color). The Romantics added the category of "the sublime", which refers to a kind of wonder and awe that makes us feel humble and happy. Gothic cathedrals amazingly combine these two aspects, the rational and the "Romantic", structure and surprise, meaning and mystery.

The beauty that causes our joy is objective, not subjective. It is not "in the eye of the beholder". It is *beheld*. Yet it is beheld in individually unique ways: each beholder beholds some different aspect or angle of beauty and appreciates different beautiful objects, especially different music. That is why Dante, and no one else, fell in love with Beatrice. But the beauty was in her, not in him.

The Iroquois word *orenda* designates the beauties of nature that move us and give us joy even though we cannot use them, only admire them—especially stars, mountains, forests, rivers, and seas. It is a kind of spiritual magnetism that draws us out of ourselves, as self-forgetful love does.

If God is the Author and archetype of all beauty, as well as of all truth and goodness, it follows that the finite beauties that are the greatest are those that are the most Godlike. And these are the beauty of truth and goodness. Among all concrete creatures, the most beautiful is Mary. We say to her, "*Tota pulchra es*"—"You are *wholly* beautiful", absolutely "*full* of grace". All beauty, like all being, is a grace from God: a deliberately created gift. "Grace" means "style" as well as "gift", like a Michael Jordan steal, fake, and slam dunk.

Animals can also elicit our joy by their beauty, which is very varied and often strange (armadillos, platypuses, angelfish), lordly (lions, tigers, eagles), or funny (giraffes, ostriches, gooney birds, meerkats, beetles). One reason God created them is to give us mirrors in which we could see ourselves and laugh at ourselves; this, in turn, is one of the most delightful of joys.

90

Art as a Cause of Our Joy

We can *make* beauty by our arts as well as contemplate and appreciate it. This increases our joy in two ways: it adds to the stock of beautiful things in the universe, and it fulfills and perfects a power in our souls, the power not just to know and love but also to make, to create—not, as God creates, out of nothing but out of something. We make because we are made in the image of the Maker. Art is part of the image of God in us.

All art creates beauty, even when it deliberately creates ugliness: it is the beauty of ugliness, ugliness deliberately affirmed and appreciated, like Eeyore in *Winnie-the-Pooh* or like basset hounds.

Art's highest function is to give us joy through creating more beauty for us to contemplate and enjoy, as a little appetizer for the Beatific Vision. For God is beauty as well as truth and goodness. He is the beauty *of* truth and goodness. Truth and goodness do not merely *exist*; they *shine*, in both God and man, in both nature and art. The greatest material work of art is the universe itself. That is why science can be a great cause of joy. Science is the human mind's great work of divine art appreciation.

The greatest joy art can give is the joy that manifests itself in tears. "You break my heart": no greater compliment can be given to an artist. To understand why opposite spiritual feelings (great joy and great sorrow) generate identical physical manifestations (tears), read C. S. Lewis' essay "Transposition".

The two arts that seem to cause the deepest joy are music and architecture, for opposite reasons: music, by being liquid and moving like the waves of the sea; architecture by being solid and remaining like the rocks of the land. Music moves us because it moves; architecture moves us because it stands.

The key to appreciating either a great cathedral or a great symphony is to get inside it, both physically and spiritually. When you are inside a great cathedral, you feel you are already in Heaven. When you listen aright to a great symphony, you are not outside it, looking in, but are inside it, looking out, looking at the world differently; the music gives you new eyes. When you are part of a chorus singing Handel's *Messiah*, you experience a double joy: you are contemplating and appreciating a work already done (Handel's), and you are also creating a new thing, a performance. Oral cultures see writing as secondary, as something like mere directions (like sheet music) for a performance, and they see speaking as a performance art. There is something to that, for there is certainly more joy in hearing a symphony performed than in imagining it from just reading the score. I suspect that if there are books in Heaven, they come alive as they often do in the Harry Potter movies.

What do we see and enjoy in a great cathedral or a great symphony? An image, in stone or in sound, of human life as a whole. We usually experience and understand each part of a large whole like the universe itself separately and partially, and we do not see the "big picture". But in great art each part is integrated with each other part and with the whole so that even the gargoyles and the dissonances fit, as, in our lives, even the accidents and the tragedies fit from a God's-eye point of view. In cathedrals and music, we share that God's-eye point of view.

But the greatest art, the greatest work of creation, that we can possibly accomplish is procreation, in which we supply the body for which God creates a new eternal soul. Mothers are the greatest artists in the world. And therefore, Mary, who procreated God Incarnate, is not only the greatest art but also the greatest artist.

91

Music as a Cause of Our Joy

I think the most joyful appreciation of music comes from focusing on one great composer, as you would focus on one person to fall in love with. (Music is like romance in many ways.) For me, it is Giovanni Palestrina. The first time I heard him, I knew with certainty that this was heavenly music, not earthly music. It was an echo of the music Adam and Eve heard in the Garden of Eden before the Fall, when God walked with them hand in hand, heart in heart, and face-to-face in the cool of the evening. Palestrina's music was only a very faint echo of that primal music, because it came down through many centuries of time; but it clearly came from above, not from within. It was extraterrestrial, like an angel. It was to the human voice what Fra Angelico is to painting and what Chopin is to the piano.

But to hear this, you must listen. To receive it is an active act, like catching a baseball. Listening, whether to music or to people or to God, is essential to joy. Abandon all utilitarian intentions. When you listen to the music that captures and raptures your heart, you are not solving a puzzle or passing a test or learning a lesson. You are not doing it to attain any future goal; the whole of you is in the present, en-joying it, basking in it. If there is any future reference, it is an eschatological prophecy of the harmony of all things that we will see and understand when God lets us enter the porches of His mind. Music suggests this better than any other art. There is an old tradition that the language God spoke to create the world, and the language spoken in Eden and before Babel, was music. (See Tolkien's *The Silmarillion* and C. S. Lewis' *The Magician's Nephew*.)

Music is like the ocean, and we are like its beaches. Music, like everything physical, comes in waves. Music is essentially temporal, like everything in nature, even our minds. (It takes time to change our minds just as much as it takes time to change our clothes.) Music is movement, yet it smells of eternity. Perhaps this is because what is eternal is not something static, like a Platonic Idea, but something dynamic, the very act (not just the fact) of existing, temporally or eternally. Perhaps God is omnipresent not because He does not move but because His movement is so infinitely fast that He is in all places at once.

Our lives are musics. A piece of music, like a life, is a story. When we read great literature, the words let us visually imagine the story in our minds; when we hear great music, the sound lets us emotionally hear the story in sound, in our ears, in our bodies. Life combines the events that are the lyrics with the music that is the score. Take a movie whose music is haunting—*The Last of the Mohicans*, for instance. Jarring music appropriate to a slasher movie would radically reinterpret and misunderstand both the events and the characters in that movie. In life, the events are like history, and music is like philosophy. Philosophy is life's hermeneutics (the science of interpretation). Heaven will be vastly improved "music appreciation". We will understand and interpret the events and the characters through God's musical score.

Tolkien's Creation story at the beginning of *The Silmarillion* is called the "Ainulindalë", the "music of the

angels". In that myth ("myth" does not mean a mist or
a miss or a mistake but a sacred story), God (Eru Ilúvatar,
"All-Father") first creates musicians (the Ainur, angels) and
reveals to them a music—His music—and then it becomes
the cosmos, when He commands it to "be" (the commanding word of Creation) and become history, in which the
music plays out. When evil's cacophony interrupts Eru's
harmony, He integrates the disharmony into the higher
harmony. History is "His story", and in its music, the
Devil's two supreme triumphs of death and destruction,
the Fall and the Crucifixion, become triumphant notes
in the great symphony of Romans 8:28.

92

Humor as a Cause of Our Joy

Why do we laugh? No animal does. There are no such things as "laughing hyenas" any more than there are "wise owls".

When we laugh with the belly as well as with the brain, our joy takes us over (overtakes us) and moves both our hearts and our bodies in a way that physically resembles delirium tremens, fear, terror, indigestion, hiccups, or orgasm. We are no longer in control. We are under a spell. We shake because we are shaken. We are shaken and stirred because we are not drunk; we are the drink. We are both ridiculous and inspired.

And this apparent loss, a loss of control, is a great gain. It is a kind of ecstasy, in the literal sense of standing out-side oneself (*ek-stasis*). Laughter is almost a mystical experience. It is at least a clue that we are designed for mystical experience.

Good philosophers (that is, nonreductionist, nonmaterialist philosophers) usually identify the central strategy and structure of humor as *irony*, which is the contrast between appearance and reality, or expectation and result. This distinction between appearance and reality is the origin of curiosity and wonder, which is the beginning of both philosophy and science. The shock of emotional wonder leads to the inquiry of intellectual wonder, which, in turn, leads to the contemplative wonder of appreciation.

So humor, science, and philosophy all rest on the same foundation of irony. And ironically, irony is itself ironic because it means that reality is not appearance, yet reality appears!

The fact that humor, hiccups, sexual orgasm, and mystical experience share a common visible structure is itself hilariously funny because it is so ironic. That fact can edify and instruct us more effectively than sermons or arguments, for it humbles our pride (for we are tempted to be terribly "spiritual" about religion), and it takes our animal nature and its power of reproduction and makes it into an icon of mystical experience. It also makes it into the greatest and most creative thing we can do in this world—namely, to procreate eternal souls, the only things in the universe that have intrinsic and eternal value, the only things that God loves for their own sake: us. That explains why we laugh the most at religious and sexual jokes: because they are surprisingly similar, for both are at once very serious and very funny. Without losing any of its seriousness, religion is the funniest thing in the world, especially God's joke on Satan at Calvary. And without losing any of its material animality, sex is the most creative and Godlike power in the world. It is also both ironic and hilarious that in designing us, God identified the organ of sexual ecstasy with the organ of garbage disposal. We cannot help laughing at this joke on our pride, and there are few things healthier, happier, and holier than that laugh.

Our faith makes it possible for us to laugh at the most humorless being in existence, the Devil, and at his supreme triumph, death: "'O death, where is your victory? O death, where is your sting?' The sting of death is sin" (1 Cor 15:55–56). Sin is the worst of all evils because it separates us from God, but the Lamb of God has taken away the sins of the world and thereby made death a stingless bee. Now we can be one with the One "who sits in the heavens [and] laughs" (Ps 2:4) at death, stick our tongues out at death, and mock it. For "Thou hast made death glorious and triumphant for through its portals we enter into the presence of the Living God" ("Open Our Eyes" oratorio). The most terrible and most serious event in history is also its greatest joke.

93

Seven Reasons Why Purgatory
Is a Cause of Joy

Saint Catherine of Genoa, who had visions of Purgatory from God, says that Purgatory's pains are far greater than any earthly pain, because we clearly see, appreciate, regret, and bemoan the harm all our sins did to ourselves and to one another; but she also says that Purgatory's joys are far greater than any earthly joys. There are at least seven reasons for this.

The first reason is that God, who is the source of all joy, is intimately with us in our Purgatory, as our wise and loving surgeon healing His sick patient through a painful operation. The angels are His nurses.

Second, we are indubitably certain that Heaven lies at the end of our Purgatory. Everyone in the school of Purgatory graduates with honors. It is temporary, like a toilet or (a much better analogy) like labor pains. A beautiful baby is aborning! Purgatory is the beginning of Heaven, not of Hell. At its end, we will hear the most joyful of all words: "Well done, good and faithful servant;... enter into the joy of your master" (Mt 25:21).

A third reason for our joy in Purgatory is that the pain is what we will passionately *want* because after death we will want only what God wants.

In fact, we will be incapable of sinning, and that's a fourth great reason for joy in Purgatory. Our will will no longer be in any disharmony with God's will but only in passionate agreement with it; and we will know that God wills the pain, so we will will it too, not rebel against it as we instinctively do here. There will be no gap between what we want and what we get—that gap being the very definition of unhappiness.

A fifth reason for the joy is that Purgatory frees us from the heavy albatross of guilt hanging around our necks. We will feel like a knight taking off heavy armor; like a snake shedding its old, dirty, ugly skin; or like Eustace Scrubb being "de-dragoned" in C. S. Lewis' *The Voyage of the Dawn Treader*.

Or, to use a surprising but apt analogy (this counts as reason six), it will be like ending our spiritual constipation. That image is not impious, because the insulting comparison is a joke on sin and dirt, not on virtue and cleanness, and also because God designed both Purgatory and toilet training, as well as their similarity.

Reason seven is that Purgatory, like Heaven, is full of the light of truth, and truth is a joy to all who love it. When Jesus says, "You will know the truth, and the truth will make you free" (Jn 8:32), He is speaking about Purgatory. For only in Purgatory will we know the whole truth about ourselves, both the depth of darkness that is our sins (thus the pain) and also the height of the light of our salvation (thus the joy). We will know the truth; we will *see* how purifying the pain is, and we will see both its cause, God's love, and its effect, our perfection.

We can begin to enter into the joy of Purgatory now. If "all the way to Heaven is Heaven" (attributed to Saint Teresa of Avila), all the way to Purgatory is also Purgatory. We can actually en-joy, or take joy in, our sufferings now—not for themselves (we are not masochists) but for the "eternal weight of glory" that they lead to (2 Cor 4:17).

This accepting of suffering is not the pride that says, "Come on, God, give me more; I can take it!" Christ Himself teaches us to pray humbly, "Lead us not into temptation [i.e., trials]" (Mt 6:13), humbly to ask God to lighten our load because we are weak. When we sin, we say to God, "I see. That is what I always must be without Your grace."

The picture of Purgatory painted here is put perfectly in George Herbert's poem "Bitter-Sweet":

> Ah, my deare angrie Lord,
> Since thou dost love, yet strike;
> Cast down, yet help afford;
> Sure I will do the like.
>
> I will complain, yet praise;
> I will bewail, approve;
> And all my sowre-sweet days
> I will lament and love.

(And even in the lament, since I will love, I will be in joy.)

94

The Real "Joy of Sex"

The Eucharist is our supreme joy on earth because it consummates our marriage to Christ. It is "the *spiritual* marriage", yet we become "the mystical *Body* of Christ" by *physically* eating His eucharistic Body. If this sounds shocking to you, you are one with the disciples who became the first Protestants by protesting and walking away from Jesus because He spoke of Himself in this way (Jn 6:48–69). But His Jewish prophets had predicted this protest when they said, shockingly, "Your Maker is your husband" (Is 54:5).

In Holy Communion, we join Christ in a foretaste of the marriage of the Lamb and His Bride. We joy in Christ, and He joys in us. Our joy is limited by our ability to receive Him (for everything that is received is received according to the capacity of the receiver) and by our less-than-a-mustard-seed-sized faith, hope, and charity. But it is not limited by our bodies. Our whole bodies receive the whole Christ, whole-body and whole-soul.

If we saw this clearly and appreciated it aright, I think our spirits would simply explode like a supernova. It's only God's mercy that keeps us in relative ignorance, as earth's atmosphere filters the sun's rays.

No, it's not sex, or like sex, but sex is like it, by God's own design. Why is sexual intercourse so explodingly joyful? Not just because it fulfills the most passionate desire of the flesh, for it transcends anything we share with the animals. No animal is a person; therefore, no animal knows even human, personal, romantic love, much less spiritual marriage. Even human *eros* love raises sexual desire and sexual joy to a radically higher-than-animal level by personalizing the sex that has sexualized the person. On this distinctively human level, even though not yet raised to the supernatural level, the romantic lovers long to give themselves totally to each other and to be "in" each other, without losing their individual identities but rather finding them. For at what moment do lovers come into the completest possession of their deepest and most unique individual identities? At the moment they are most totally lost in each other.

The word Scripture uses for sex is "knowledge" (Gen 4:1). It is not a euphemism! The deepest thrill comes from the personal knowledge, the intimacy, the thought that this precious person whom I love with my whole being, body and soul, and to whom I give my whole self, body and soul, loves *me* with his or her whole body and soul too and invites me into himself or herself, body and soul. It is life's most sacred intimacy. The "knowing" is the joy.

As romantic love transcends and personalizes biological sex, the spiritual marriage transcends and supernaturalizes romantic love. That is why sex is so sacred, so holy (and therefore also so unholy when perverted: *corruptio optimi pessima*): because total self-giving (*agape*) is the height of love—and of joy. Physical sexual desire is the most intense *bodily* joy. Romantic love is the most intense *emotional* joy. *Agape* love is the greatest *spiritual* joy, and this is the greatest joy of all because it is the very nature and life of God the Holy Trinity. Like God Himself, *agape* is the maximum: maximum love and maximum joy. And that is the love we participate in through Holy Communion.

One last time, I seem to hear the fallen voices of misery whispering in your ear and objecting, "But you don't *feel* anything like that!" If that is your objection, you are as big a fool as the murderer who, after being tried and convicted, objected to the judge, "But, Your Honor, I don't *feel* guilty." Your feelings are your god, your idol. Grow up! Throw away your fake-joy machine. The real God, the true God, is waiting for you.

95

The Three Most Essential Sources of Joy

It took me eighty-seven years to get to the point of under-standing (1) that everything we do and say is done or said to God—in other words, is prayer—and (2) that there are only three prayers we need to pray. Everything is in these prayers. Nothing we need is outside them.

1. "Thy will be done."
2. "Jesus, I trust in You."
3. "Come, Holy Spirit."

Less is more.

CONCLUSION

Those ninety-five pensées were the second of the three points of my three-point sermon. The introduction was the first. Here is the third.

Joy wins because God wins. Sorrow is always squeezed between two joys, God as Alpha and God as Omega—always, everywhere, necessarily. For whatever things or events are the causes of our sorrow and suffering, they began with the beginning of all things and events when God created the universe. As every atom in our bodies is made of "star stuff", every event in our lives is made of "divine providence stuff". And God the Alpha, the Creator and the beginning of all things, who is joy, works all things and events in the plot of the Greatest Story—even the acts of His stupid and wicked characters—toward a single end, which is joy, because God is Omega as well as Alpha. He is the Mind of infinite, all-inclusive Wisdom and the Will of infinite, all-inclusive Love. Nothing escapes the plot of that story because there is no other place than that story, the story of All Things in the History of the Universe, for anything to go to get existence.

God is more than just, because justice is finite, but mercy is infinite. That's where all the things that came to you came from: infinite Love and Mercy. (Sins did not come to you; they came from you.) He is also where all things lead to: to the same God whom infinite Love came from.

Even the cross. Especially the cross—His large one and our small ones, which are like tiny toys made out of the wood of the large one. In the Middle Ages, there were so many false relics of the true cross that one wag estimated that if they were all real, Noah's ark could have been made out of them. Well, the joke is on the wag, because *all* our crosses are true crosses, shards of His cross. If we are Christians—i.e., if we are "in" Christ, members (organs!) of His Body—then all our crosses are made out of the real cross. Christ says both "Take *my* yoke upon you" and "If any man would come after me, let him deny himself and take up *his* cross and follow me" (Mt 11:29; 16:24, emphasis added), proving that our crosses are His and His is ours. That's what love does: it makes everything that is mine yours and everything that is yours mine.

The snaky python called Satan squeezed the life out of our joy in Eden, but Christ squeezed away the sorrow by surrounding it with joy so that our crosses, our sorrows, are now, in fact, servants of our joy. Of course, we do not usually feel this or see this; that's what faith is: a leap, a wager, an investment, a drama.

Christ is not our Santa Claus carrying our joy with Him in a sack as a gift. He *is* our joy; the Giver *is* the gift. And we receive that gift, in its totality and its perfection, every time we receive Him in the Eucharist.

We don't see or feel that either. So why do we believe it? Is it a leap in the dark? No, it's a leap in the light. Because our God is not a liar. Too bad about all the other gods.

Yet there is a half-truth in everything the Devil says to confuse us, and there is a half-truth in his retort to all these thoughts: that though they seem beautiful on paper, our attempt to live them is a bloody mess of a war against the forces of selfishness, joylessness, faithlessness, hopelessness, and lovelessness, which are our real enemies and which have embedded themselves in our souls like little vampires sucking our lifeblood.

Yes, but there is no war more worth winning. No price is too high to pay for divine joy. Its gain is *total* gain, and its loss is *total* loss. The quest for that joy is what Kierkegaard calls "the infinite passion."[1] The vast majority of people in our post-Christian culture have absolutely no idea what that "infinite passion" means, and they classify it as "religious fanaticism". I have nothing but compassion for that lack of passion. That is why I try to share the Good News with them, however incomprehensible, discombobulating, discomforting, and even terrifying it may be. Why is it that? Because Christ is not only "the *Lamb* of God" but also "the *Lion* of the tribe of Judah" (Jn 1:36; Rev 5:5, emphasis added). He is Christ the Lion, not Christ the kitten. As they say of Aslan in Narnia, " 'Course he isn't *safe*. But he's *good*."[2] For He is love, and love is not safe. In fact, it is excruciating. But it is our supreme joy.

Do it! Be a saint. What else is there?

[1] Søren Kierkegaard, *Concluding Unscientific Postscript to Philosophical Crumbs*, ed. and trans. Alastair Hannay (Cambridge: Cambridge University Press, 2009), 18.

[2] C. S. Lewis, *The Lion, the Witch and the Wardrobe* (New York: Harper-Collins, 1950), 86, emphasis added.